DATE			

Chapter Two

CHAPTER TWO

A NEW COMEDY BY

Neil Simon

RANDOM HOUSE   NEW YORK

Grateful acknowledgment is made to the following for permission to reprint previously published material:
Warner Bros. Inc., lyrics from "The Man I Love" by Ira Gershwin. Copyright © 1924 New World Music Corp. Copyright renewed. All rights reserved. Used by permission of Warner Bros. Music.
Tempo Music, Inc. and Edwin H. Morris and Co., lyrics from "Flamingo" by Ted Grouya. Copyright © 1941 by Tempo Music, Inc. Copyright renewed, assigned to Edwin H. Morris & Co., a Division of MPL Communications, Inc.
Library of Congress Cataloging in Publication Data
Simon, Neil.
    Chapter two.
    I. Title.
PS3537.I663C48   812'.5'4   78-57093
ISBN 0-394-50293-0

Manufactured in the United States of America

2 3 4 5 6 7 8 9

First Edition

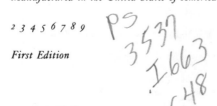

To Marsha

CHAPTER TWO *was first presented on December 4, 1977, by Emanuel Azenberg at the Imperial Theatre, New York City, with the following cast:*

GEORGE SCHNEIDER	Judd Hirsch
LEO SCHNEIDER	Cliff Gorman
JENNIE MALONE	Anita Gillette
FAYE MEDWICK	Ann Wedgeworth

Directed by Herbert Ross
Scenery by William Ritman
Lighting by Tharon Musser
Costumes by Noel Taylor

THE SCENE

The action of *Chapter Two* takes place in Jennifer Malone's upper East Side apartment and George Schneider's lower Central Park West apartment. The play begins on a late February afternoon and continues through to midspring.

Act One

The set consists of two separate apartments on opposite sides of Manhattan—GEORGE SCHNEIDER *lives in one;* JENNIE MALONE, *in the other.*

His apartment, stage left, is located in the mid-seventies on Central Park West. It is one of New York's older buildings, and the ceilings and rooms are higher and larger than the smaller, flatter, uninteresting boxes they build today.

Hers is one of the smaller, flatter, uninteresting boxes they build today. It is in the upper eighties off Third Avenue.

His is decorated in a traditional, comfortable style—large inviting armchairs and sofa, bookcases from floor to ceiling, lots of personal photographs of him and his wife.

Hers is modern, bright, attractive and cheerful. That's because she is.

We see the living rooms of both apartments plus the entrance doors. His apartment has a kitchen and an archway that leads into four other rooms. Hers has a small kitchen and single bedroom.

It's about 10:30 P.M. *in his apartment. The door opens and* GEORGE SCHNEIDER *enters. He wears a coat and scarf and carries a large fully packed leather suitcase and an attaché case. He turns on the lights.* GEORGE *is forty-two years old, an attractive, intelligent man who at this moment seems tired and drawn. He puts down his bags, looks around the room, and goes over to a table where his mail has been placed. A large number of letters have piled up. He goes through them, throwing every second and third piece into the wastebasket;*

3

*the rest he takes with him to a chair, where he sits and starts
to look through them.*

LEO SCHNEIDER *appears, carrying* GEORGE*'s other match-
ing suitcase.* LEO *is about forty. He is wearing a suede sheep-
skin coat, scarf and gloves.*

LEO *(Coming through the door)* George, you're not
going to believe this! I found a place to park right
in front of the building. First time in four years
. . . I think I'll buy an apartment here—I don't want
to give up that space. *(Puts the suitcase down)* Christ
Almighty, it's four degrees in here. Whooo! Whyn't
you rent it out for the winter Olympics, pay your
expenses. Where do you turn your heat on? *(*GEORGE
is reading his mail) I smell gas. Do you smell gas,
George?

GEORGE *(Looks up)*   What?

LEO   *Gas,* for Chrissakes! *(He runs into the kitchen, to the
stove.* GEORGE *continues to read his mail.* LEO *comes out)*
It was on. Didn't you check it before you left?
Thank God I didn't have a cigar on me. One match,
we'd *both* be back in Italy. *(Turns on the desk lamp)*
Where do you turn the heat on? . . . *George?*

GEORGE   What?

LEO   Where is the heater?

GEORGE   The heater? It's, uh . . .

LEO   Take your time. Accuracy is important.

4

GEORGE   I'm sorry . . . The thermostat's on the wall as you come in the bedroom.

LEO *(Looks at him)*   Are you all right?

GEORGE   No. Am I supposed to be?

LEO   You lost weight, didn't you?

GEORGE   I don't know. A couple of pounds.

LEO   Sure. Who could eat that lousy food in Paris and Rome?

GEORGE   Do you smell gas?

LEO   What?

GEORGE   I smell gas.

LEO   I think your nose is having jet lag, George.
(He goes into the bedroom)

GEORGE   I was going to stay another week in Rome. Then I said, "No, I have to get back. I'm really anxious to be home." *(He looks around)* I wonder why I thought that.

LEO *(Reentering)*   Come on. You walk into Ice Station Zebra with gas leaking in the kitchen and no fresh air in here for four and a half weeks. I mean, this is February and we're standing here breathing January . . . Why don't you make some popcorn, see what's on TV.
(He takes the suitcases into the bedroom. GEORGE *shakes his head)*

GEORGE   God!

LEO *(Enters)*   You've got to see the bathroom. You left the shower dripping with the little window wide open. There are icicles hanging everywhere. It's beautiful. It looks like the john in *Doctor Zhivago* . . . What are you reading?

GEORGE   My mail.

LEO   Anything interesting?

GEORGE   Not unless you like letters of condolence. I thought I answered my last one when I left . . . Do we have an Aunt Henry?

LEO *(Offstage)*   *Aunt* Henry? We have an *Uncle* Henry. In Kingston, New York.

GEORGE   This is signed "Aunt Henry."

LEO *(Offstage)*   Uncle Henry's about sixty-three— maybe he's going through a change of life.

GEORGE *(Reading)*   " 'Sorry to hear about your loss. With deepest sincerity, Aunt Henry.' "

LEO *(Comes out of the kitchen; holding up the food)*   You want to see sour milk? You want to see white bread that's turned into pumpernickel all by itself? You want to see a dish of grapes that have dried into raisins?

GEORGE *(Looking at another letter)*   You want to listen to something, Leo?

LEO *(Trying to avoid the past)* George, you just got home. You're tired. Why don't you defrost the bathroom, take a bath?

GEORGE Just one letter: "Dear Mr. Schneider, My name is Mary Ann Patterson. We've never met, but I did know your late wife, Barbara, casually. I work at Sabrina's, where she used to come to have her hair cut. She was so beautiful and one of the warmest people I've ever met. It seems I always used to tell her my troubles, and she always found some terrific thing to say to cheer me up. I will miss her smiling face and the way she used to come bouncing into the shop like a little girl. I feel lucky to have known her. I just wanted to return a little of her good cheer. God bless you and keep you. Mary Ann Patterson." *(He puts down the letter.* LEO *looks at him, knowing not to intrude on this moment)* What the hell did I read *that* for?

LEO It's very nice. It's a sweet letter, George.

GEORGE Barbara knew a whole world of people I never knew . . . She knew that Ricco, the mailman, was a birdwatcher in Central Park, and that Vince, the butcher in Gristede's, painted miniature portraits of cats every weekend in his basement on Staten Island . . . She talked to people all year long that I said hello to on Christmas.

LEO *(Looks at him)* I think you could have used another month in Europe.

GEORGE   You mean, I was supposed to come home and forget I had a wife for twelve years? It doesn't work that way, Leo. It was, perhaps, the dumbest trip I ever took in my whole life. London was bankrupt, Italy was on strike, France hated me, Spain was still mourning for Franco . . . Why do Americans go to grief-stricken Europe when they're trying to get over being stricken with grief?

LEO   Beats me. I always thought you could have just as rotten a time here in America.

GEORGE   What am I going to do about this apartment, Leo?

LEO   My advice? Move. Find a new place for yourself.

GEORGE   It was very spooky in London . . . I kept walking around the streets looking for Barbara—Harrod's, King's Road, Portobello . . . Sales clerks would say, "See what you want, sir?" and I'd say, "No, she's not here." I know it's crazy, Leo, but I really thought to myself, It's a joke. She's not dead. She's in London waiting for me. She's just playing out this romantic fantasy: The whole world thinks she's gone, but we meet clandestinely in London, move into a flat, disappear from everyone and live out our lives in secret! . . . She would have thought of something like that, you know.

LEO   But she didn't. *You* did.

GEORGE   In Rome I got sore at her—I mean *really* mad. How dare she do a thing like this to me? I

8

would *never* do a thing like that to her. Never! Like a nut, walking up the Via Veneto one night, cursing my dead wife.

LEO   In Italy, they probably didn't pay attention.

GEORGE   In Italy, they agree with you. *(He shrugs)* Okay, Leo, my sweet baby brother, I'm back . . . Chapter Two in the life of George Schneider. Where the hell do I begin?

LEO   I don't know. You want to go to a dance?

GEORGE   You know, you're cute. Does Marilyn think you're cute?

LEO   Yeah. It's not enough. I want *all* the women to think so.

GEORGE   Everything okay at home?

LEO   Couldn't be better.

GEORGE   You sure?

LEO   Never ask a question like that twice. I gotta go. *(He buttons his coat)* How about poker on Thursday?

GEORGE   I'll let you know.

LEO   Want me to get tickets for the Knicks game Saturday?

GEORGE   We'll talk about it.

LEO   How about dinner on Sunday? Monday? Maybe Tuesday will be my good news day? *(Imitates a trom-*

bone playing "The Man I Love." GEORGE *doesn't respond)* Hey! Hey, Georgie . . .

GEORGE   I'm okay, Leo. I promise. Just give me a little time, okay?

LEO   I don't know what to do for you . . . I feel so goddamn helpless.

GEORGE   Well . . . Maybe you can come by tomorrow and show me how to open up tuna fish.

LEO *(Looks at* GEORGE *)*   Now *I'm* mad. I think it stinks, too. I'm not going to forgive her for a long time, George. (LEO *goes over and embraces* GEORGE. *Tears well up in* LEO*'s eyes. He pulls away and heads for the door)* I'm coming back next week and the two of us are getting bombed, you understand? I mean, I want you *disgusting!* Then we'll drive up to Kingston and check out this Aunt Henry. If he's got money, he might be a nice catch for you.
   (He turns and goes quickly. GEORGE *turns and looks at the apartment, then picks up his attaché case)*

GEORGE *(He takes in a deep breath)*   Okay, let's take it one night at a time, folks.
   (He heads for the bedroom. The lights come down slowly)

Scene 2

Her apartment. It is mid-February, about four-thirty on a bitter-cold afternoon. The light of a winter's day is fading fast.

The door opens and JENNIE MALONE *enters and switches on the lights. She is an attractive woman, about thirty-two. She wears a camel's-hair coat, leather boots and a woolen hat. She puts down a valise and carries a heavily loaded shoulder bag. She looks around and exhales a deep sigh.*

Right behind her is FAYE MEDWICK, *about thirty-five.* FAYE *dresses a bit more suburban—not chic, but right for the weather. She carries in* JENNIE *'s make-up case.*

FAYE   I don't care *how* much traffic there was, no way is it twenty-six dollars from Kennedy Airport to Eighty-fourth Street. *(She closes the door)* It's one thing to pay for his gas, it's another to put his daughter through college. (JENNIE *takes off her coat*) Remember that cabbie last year? Picked up this sweet Mexican family at the airport, drove them into the city and charged them *a hundred and sixty dollars?* He told them in America the cab fare starts from the time you get on the plane. I could kill sometimes . . . It's nice and warm in here. You left the heat on for two weeks?

JENNIE   I told the doorman I was coming back today. He probably turned it on this morning.

11

FAYE Organized. You're so damn organized. I'd give anything to be like you. I'm hungry. We should have stopped off at the grocery.
(She enters the kitchen)

JENNIE I dropped an order off with them before I left. They may have delivered it this morning.

FAYE *(Opens the fridge, looks in)* It's all there! Jesus! You fly two thousand miles to get a divorce and you remember to leave a grocery order?

JENNIE *(Dials the phone)* It's that Catholic upbringing. I majored in Discipline.

FAYE Milk, cheese, butter, eggs, bread . . . Listen, would you like a job in my house? Your own room with color TV?

JENNIE A perfect person. The nuns loved it, but it was murder on a marriage. *(Into the phone)* Four-six-two, please.

FAYE Your plants look nice too. Had them watered, right?

JENNIE Three times a week. *(Into the phone)* Yes?

FAYE You have the nerve to tell that to a woman with a dead lawn and two fallen trees?

JENNIE *(Into the phone)* Thank you. *(Hangs up)* I'm going to change my answering service. I get such boring messages.

FAYE Is there *anything* you forgot?

JENNIE Nothing. I've got everything planned up until five o'clock. Starting at 5:01—help! If it's so warm in here, why am I shivering?

FAYE You just cut off six years of your life. Giggling would be inappropriate.

JENNIE I can still smell the ghost of Gus's cigar. God, what a cheap thing to be haunted by . . . He probably came by to pick up the rest of his clothes.

FAYE Sidney's been complaining the dry cleaner I use does terrible work. I haven't got the nerve to tell him I keep forgetting to send it out.

JENNIE Y'know, I never realized I had so many books I never read . . . Okay, *Catch-22*, we're going to try it one more time.

FAYE You see, I think that's wrong. To tackle heavyweight material is not what you should be doing now. I would read filth.

JENNIE Listen, you're not going to hang around till I've readjusted, are you, Faye?

FAYE Well, you've got to go slowly. I don't want you to get the bends. *(Looking out the window)* Oh, God!

JENNIE What?

FAYE I'm watching the most gorgeous naked person across the street.

JENNIE Man or woman?

FAYE Can't tell. It's a rear view.

JENNIE That's probably Lupe, the Spanish dancer. Beautiful body.

FAYE Fantastic. Women are really terrific. No wonder we drive men crazy . . . some of us . . . Did you ever fantasize making love to a beautiful woman?

JENNIE You're not going to make any advances, are you, Faye? I'm really very tired.

FAYE It's just that sometimes I watch Sidney drooling over those Dallas Cowboy cheerleaders, and I was wondering what I was missing in life . . . Maybe I never should have left Texas.

JENNIE What's wrong this week?

FAYE Sidney and I had dinner with friends last week. A couple married twenty years, the man never stopped fondling his wife for a minute. They both said it was the best time of their lives—that they really never knew how to enjoy each other till now. And I thought to myself, "Shit. Twelve more years to go until the good times."

JENNIE Did you tell that to Sidney?

FAYE *(Putting on her coat)* Not yet. I can't get an appointment with his secretary.

JENNIE I don't understand you. I know more about what's wrong with your married life than Sidney does. Why don't you speak up? What are you afraid of? What do you think would happen to you if you told him what you tell *me* in the privacy of this room?

FAYE   That next time you'd be picking *me* up at the airport.

JENNIE   Oh, God, that infuriates me. Why are we so intimidated? I wasted five lousy years living with Gus trying to justify the one good year I had with him . . . because I wouldn't take responsibility for my own life. Dumb! You're dumb, Jennie Malone! *All* of us . . . We shouldn't get alimony, we should get the *years* back. Wouldn't it be great if just once the judge said, "I award you six years, three months, two days and custody of your former youthful body and fresh glowing skin"!

FAYE   I would be in such terrific shape if you were my mother.

JENNIE   Don't give me too much credit. I *talk* a terrific life . . . Now, go on home. I want to crawl into bed and try to remember what my maiden name was.

FAYE   Are you sure you'll be all right? All alone?

JENNIE   No. But I want to be.
    (*They embrace*)

FAYE   You can call me in the middle of the night. Sidney and I aren't doing anything.
    (FAYE *leaves.* JENNIE *takes her suitcase into the bedroom*)

His apartment. It is the next night, about 5 P.M. GEORGE is obviously having difficulty concentrating at the typewriter. He is wearing slacks, an open-neck shirt, woolen cardigan and slippers. The phone rings as he is typing.

GEORGE *(Into the phone)* Hello . . . Yes . . . Who's this? . . . Leona Zorn . . . Oh, yes. Yes, I received your note. I was very dismayed to hear that you and Harvey broke up . . . Well, I wouldn't say we were close friends. He's a wonderful chiropracter . . . Dinner on Thursday? Thursday . . . Thursday . . . Ah, nuts, I have something on for Thursday . . . The following Thursday? *(The doorbell rings)* Gee, I think I have something on for that night, too . . . Uh, Mrs. Zorn, will you just hold on? I want to get my doorbell. *(He lays the receiver down; under his breath)* Oh, Jesus!
   (He opens the door. LEO enters)

LEO   Sit down. I have to talk to you.

GEORGE   Just a minute, Leo, I'm on the phone. *(Into the phone)* Mrs. Zorn? . . . You said the following Thursday? . . . I think I have something on for that night, but let me check my diary. I'll be right back. *(He puts the receiver down and goes over to LEO. GEORGE beckons, gesturing that phone is "open")* Leo, there's a woman on the phone asking me for a date.

16

LEO   Yeah? . . . So?

GEORGE *(Whispers)* Her husband was my chiropracter.

LEO   So what?

GEORGE   He left her for an ice-skater in Las Vegas.

LEO   What does she look like?

GEORGE   Like someone you would leave for an ice-skater in Las Vegas.

LEO   So what's your problem?

GEORGE *(Annoyed)* What do you mean, what's my problem? I don't want to have dinner with her.

LEO   What *do* you want to have?

GEORGE   *Nothing!* I want her to hang up. I don't want her to call me. Look, she's probably a very nice woman. I don't want to be cruel to her, but I don't want to have dinner with her.

LEO   Would you feel better if *I* took her out? What's her name? I'll talk to her.
       (GEORGE *stops him*)

GEORGE   Leo! Please! *(Back into the phone)* Mrs. Zorn? . . . I'm sorry to keep you waiting . . . Uh, Mrs. Zorn, I've always found it better to be completely honest . . . and . . . I'm really not all that anxious to go out at this particular time . . . Well, I've tried it a few times and it wasn't all that successful . . . I just don't think I'm psychologically ready . . . Well, I don't

think I can give an exact date when I *would* be ready
. . . (LEO *does push-ups on the floor*) Well, yes, in a
manner of speaking, we *are* in the same boat . . . But
we don't necessarily have to paddle together . . . I
think we have to go up our own streams.

LEO   Jesus!

GEORGE   Well, yes, it *is* possible we could meet up-
river one day, I don't rule that out.

LEO   Is that from *The African Queen?*
(GEORGE *pulls the receiver away so* LEO*'s remark will
not be heard*)

GEORGE   Leo, please! (Into phone) Yes . . . Yes . . . Well,
you sound charming too . . . Well, if I *do* reconsider,
I *will* call . . . Yes. Goodbye. *(He hangs up)* Christ!
The guy leaves me with a bad back and *his* wife!

LEO   *(Gets up)*   There just aren't enough men to go
around. I *want* to help out, but Marilyn doesn't
understand.

GEORGE   Women call me up, Leo. *Women!* They call
me up on the *phone.*

LEO   What else would they call you up on?

GEORGE   But they're so *frank* about it. So open. They
just come right out with it. "How do you do. I've
been recently widowed myself." Or, "Hi! I'm a
divorcee." "I'm legally separated." "I'm *il*legally
separated." One woman called, I swear to God, I
think her husband was just on vacation.

LEO It's a competitive world, George. The woman who sits waiting by the phone sits waiting by the phone.

GEORGE Do you know I've been invited to three class reunions at schools I never even went to?

LEO Listen, George, next to Christmas, loneliness is the biggest business in America.

GEORGE Do you realize how much courage it must have taken for that woman to call me up just now?

LEO And you think you were the first and only one she's called? She probably has her husband's entire list of clients. If she called you, she's only up to the "Georges."

GEORGE And you don't find that sad?

LEO Certainly I find it sad. That's why they have game shows on TV . . . Now, if you want to feel sorry for yourself and everyone else in the world who's suffered a loss, that's your concern. It is *my* job to brighten up the place. I am God's interior decorator, and he has sent me to paint you two coats of happiness.

GEORGE Leo, don't do this to me again!

LEO This is different. This girl requires a serious discussion. I think I found buried treasure, George. Hear me out.

GEORGE I haven't recovered from *last* week's buried treasure . . . All right, it's my own fault. I should have known in that first phone conversation with her. Three "honeys," two "sugars" and one "babe" was a sure tip-off . . . I'm very busy, Leo. I've written three hundred pages of my new book and I haven't thought of a story yet.

LEO All right, I apologize. I misunderstood. I just thought you wanted someone to have a good time with.

GEORGE Look at me, Leo. I'm a nice, plain, regular person who eats fruit and wears slippers. What makes you think I'm going to like a jazzy blonde who dyes a zigzag streak of dark-blue in her hair? She looked like the cover of a record album.

LEO But a terrific body. You've got to admit that body was put together by someone who's very close to God.

GEORGE I booked a table in one of the finest French restaurants in New York. I put on a nice blue suit, rang her doorbell and this creature from *Star Wars* says hello. You know what kind of a dress she was wearing? Electric! I didn't see where it was plugged in *but this was an electric dress*! I swear to God, we got in and the cab driver got static on his radio. In the restaurant I *prayed* for another blackout.

LEO Did I tell you to take her someplace nice? Putz! You take her to the Rainbow Room, somewhere that only out-of-towners go. But you had a good time, right? Right, George? C'mon, will ya. I went to a lot of trouble. Tell me you had a good time.

GEORGE What do you mean, I had a good time? A thunderstorm came up, and I'm sitting there with a lightning rod. I did not have a good time. She ordered a nine-dollar goose-liver pâté and made a hero sandwich out of it . . . Go home, Leo.

LEO George, I have set that girl up with some very heavy clients from Hollywood, and they've been very nice to me every Christmas.

GEORGE Are you telling me she's a hooker? Are you telling me that outlet from Con Edison is a pro?

LEO Would I do that to you? My brother? Bambi's a terrific girl. A little flashy on the exterior, yes. A little Art Deco around the wardrobe, yes. But no hooker . . . Why? Did she charge you anything?

GEORGE For what? I was wet, I was afraid to touch her.

LEO Bad move on my part, okay? Some like 'em hot, some like 'em milk and cookies. I know better now. But if you're telling me you're ready for a serious woman, George, I met her last night at "21."

GEORGE Close the door on your way out, Leo.

LEO I have a feeling about this, George. Don't deny me my feelings.

GEORGE *(Starting into the bedroom)* Leo, *please!* I have my work. I have my friends. I have the Knicks, the Giants and the Mets. I have jogging and I have watercolors. My life is full. There are no more Barbaras left in the world. If you meet them *once* in your life, God has been more than good to you . . . I *will* go out. I *will* meet people. But I have to find them in my own time, in my own way. I love you for what you're doing . . . but don't do it anymore.

LEO At least let me describe her—a nose, a couple of eyes, one or two ears! *(Following* GEORGE *into the bedroom)* Let me leave her number. You don't have to call her right away. Whenever you feel like it!
(Dimout)

SCENE 4

Her apartment. A suitcase is on the sofa; JENNIE *is packing. The phone rings. She answers it.*

JENNIE Hello? . . . Well, what a surprise. How are you, Gus? . . . Fine . . . And how does it feel to be an ex-husband? . . . It's been a long time since I heard your "bachelor" voice. You got your old *pizzazz* back . . . Oh, I found an old pair of your basketball sneakers in the closet, did you want them? . . . Thanks, I can wear them to go shopping . . . *I* sound *down?* . . . Oh, I guess a combination of post-divorce blues and the Mexican water . . . I'm not sure. I've got three more weeks on the soap. I've got an offer to go to Washington and do a year of rep at the Arena Theatre . . . And you? . . . Well, hang in, you always come up with something . . . It was very sweet of you to call, Gus . . . Well, I wish you every happiness, too. This has been the nicest talk we've had in a long time . . . I will . . . *Gus!* . . . I just wanted to say—I'm sorry!
(*On the verge of tears, she hangs up. The doorbell rings; she answers it. It is* FAYE)

FAYE Do you believe in miracles?

JENNIE Do you believe in saying hello?

FAYE   Well, two miracles happened last night at "21." The producer of *As the World Turns* saw me at our table, called me today and offered me a part—

JENNIE   Congratulations! Oh, Faye, that's fantastic! Well, what's the part?

FAYE   Her name is Jarlene Indigo.

JENNIE   Jarlene Indigo?

FAYE   She's the new cellist with the Boston Symphony.

JENNIE   I love it. Will you have to learn to play?

FAYE   By Monday.

JENNIE   *(Continues her packing)*   What's the second miracle?

FAYE   Do you remember that fellow Leo Schneider who came over to our table to say hello? Sidney doesn't know, but I used to date Leo when I first got to New York. Anyway, he's got this brother, George. He's recently widowed, about forty-two, forty-three years old I think . . . You're not listening. What are you doing?

JENNIE   I am packing. If you don't know this is packing, how will you learn to play a cello?

FAYE   Where are you going?

JENNIE   Home. To Cleveland. I just have an overwhelming desire to sleep in my old, tiny bed.

FAYE   How long will you be gone?

JENNIE   A couple of days—maybe a couple of weeks.

FAYE   In Cleveland a couple of days are a couple of weeks. Can't you postpone it? Leo was going to try to get George Schneider to call this week.

JENNIE   Faye, how many times must I tell you? I don't feel like dating right now.

FAYE   Well, that's perfect. Neither does George Schneider. At least you have something in common.

JENNIE   I wonder what it is that holds our friendship together.

FAYE   He's a writer. A novelist, I think. I met him once a few years ago. Not gorgeous, but sweet-looking. With a very intelligent face.

JENNIE   Faye, please stop. I appreciate what you're doing. You and Sidney have been wonderful. I loved the dinner at "21," and the date you fixed me up with was unusual but charming.

FAYE   It's all right. I know you didn't like him.

JENNIE   It's not that I didn't like him. I couldn't *see* him. The man was six feet eight inches tall. All I could think of at dinner was what if we got married and I had a baby? I'd be giving birth for days.

FAYE   If you're going to look for things, you can find fault with everyone.

JENNIE I don't think being uncomfortable with a man who was taller than the waiter *sitting down* is looking to find fault.

FAYE I'm talking about everyone you go out with. You sit there and scrutinize them.

JENNIE I scrutinize?

FAYE Your eyes burn little holes in them. That poor fellow last night kept checking to see if his fly was open.

JENNIE All right. I won't scrutinize if you'll stop arranging my social life for me. I told you it's not important to me—why do you do it?

FAYE I don't do it for you. I do it for me.

JENNIE What?

FAYE I have visions of arranging the perfect romance for you. Someone with a dark tragic background— Jay Gatsby . . . Irving Thalberg . . . Leon Trotsky . . .

JENNIE Jesus, do I have to live out my life with *your* fantasy?

FAYE What the hell, I'm arranging it, I might as well pick who I like . . . I don't understand, Jennie. Are you telling me you're never dating again?

JENNIE *(Putting on her coat)* Yes. YES! I have dated and I have gone to parties and I have had it. If one more man greets me at the door with his silk shirt unbuttoned to his tanned navel, his chest hair neatly combed, and wearing more jewelry around his neck than me, I am turning celibate. . . . I am going to spend the rest of my life doing good work in the theatre. I am going to read all the classics starting with *Agamemnon* . . . I'll work out my sex life the best I can. And don't think I'm not worried. Sometimes I lie in bed thinking, Is it physically possible if you don't have sex for a long, long time, you can go back to being a virgin? Well, I'll find out. But first I'll find out in Cleveland.

(She grabs her suitcase and starts out. The phone rings)

FAYE   Oh, my God, maybe that's George Schneider.

JENNIE   It's *your* fantasy, *you* answer it.
(She goes. FAYE *runs after her)*

FAYE *(Yells)   I'll give you two hundred dollars if you answer that phone!*
(But JENNIE *is gone.* FAYE *closes the door and goes)*

SCENE 5

His apartment. It is two weeks later, about 9 P.M. GEORGE walks into the living room, carrying a reference book. He looks for something at the desk and around the sofa, then goes to the phone and dials, still looking about him.

GEORGE *(Into the phone)* Marilyn? ... George ... Is Leo there? ... No, you can just yell into the bathroom ... Ask him if he remembers where he left the phone number for a Mrs. Jenkins, or Jergins, or something like that. He wrote it down and left it for me somewhere in here last week ... Jenkins, Jergins ... *(Looking through some papers)* She's the old woman he told me about who used to work for the Harvard University Library about forty years ago ... No. It's research for the book ... Would you? *(Spots a paper under the kitchen phone)* Wait a minute, Marilyn, I'm gonna put you on hold. Just a second. *(Pushes the "hold" button, gets the paper from under the kitchen phone and picks up that receiver)* Marilyn, I found it. It was right under the other phone ... Yeah ... Give Tina a kiss for me. Goodbye.

> *(He hangs up both phones and looks at the paper. He dials again ... And the phone rings in her empty apartment. Just then we hear the key in the door and JENNIE enters. She turns on the lights. The phone rings again. She puts down her suitcase and picks up the receiver)*

28

JENNIE Hello?

GEORGE Hello? Is this, uh . . . I'm sorry. I'm not sure I have your name right . . . This is George Schneider —Leo Schneider's brother? I believe he told you I would be calling you.

JENNIE George Schneider?

GEORGE The writer.

JENNIE Oh . . . God! Yes . . . George Schneider. It seemed so long ago . . . I'm sorry, you caught me at a bad time. I just got off a plane and walked in the door.

GEORGE Oh, I didn't know. I'm sorry. Can I call you back?

JENNIE Well . . . Yes, I suppose so but, er . . . I'll be very honest with you, Mr. Schneider. I'm going through sort of a transition period right now, and I'm not planning to date for a while.

GEORGE *Date?* Did Leo say I was going to call you for a date?

JENNIE Well, he said you were going to call, so I assumed—

GEORGE No, no. This wasn't a date call. I'm very surprised at Leo, Miss, er . . . Is it Jenkins or Jergins?

JENNIE Is what?

GEORGE Your name.

JENNIE   It's Malone. Jennifer Malone.

GEORGE *(Confused, looks at the paper)*   Jennifer Malone?
. . . No, that's wrong.

JENNIE   I could show you my driver's license.

GEORGE   That's not the name he gave me . . . *(He looks
on the back of the paper)* Oh, geez, it's on the other
side. I couldn't read his writing. Serene Jurgens was
the one I wanted. She's an elderly woman, about
eighty-five years old.

JENNIE   Well, you know what you want better than I
do.

GEORGE   Look, I am so embarrassed. I really was
going to call you socially. At another time. I mean,
I really was.

JENNIE   Well, let's see how it goes with Serene first.
Okay? Goodbye.
    (She hangs up)

GEORGE *(Looks at the scrap of paper)*   God damn you,
Leo, get your women straight, will ya?
    *(JENNIE takes her suitcase to the bedroom. GEORGE
    thinks a moment about what to do, then looks at the
    paper and dials again. The phone rings in her bed-
    room)*

JENNIE *(Answering it)*   Hello?

GEORGE   It's me. I'm back.

JENNIE You and the old lady didn't hit it off?

GEORGE *Now* I know who you are. The girl Leo met at "21." Jennie Malone.

JENNIE That sounds right to me.

GEORGE Anyway, I'm calling back because I wanted you to know that I got the phone numbers mixed up, and I didn't want you to think I wasn't calling you. I *was*. I mean, I wasn't *then*. I am *now*.

JENNIE For a date?

GEORGE No. Not yet. I thought I'd wait and explain the *last* call before I went ahead with the *next* call.

JENNIE I'm a little slow. Which call are we on now?

GEORGE This is the call back to explain the dumb call. The charming call comes after we hang up from this one.

JENNIE I'm so glad I'm home. If I got this message on my answering service, I'd need a private detective.

GEORGE I'll tell you the absolute truth. I haven't made a call to a nice single girl in fourteen years. I wasn't even good at it then. If I seem inept, please bear with me.

JENNIE You seem ept enough. The point is, Mister . . . er . . .

GEORGE George Schneider. I got it here on the paper.

JENNIE   The point is, Mr. Schneider, as I told Faye to tell Leo to tell you, I really have to get my head together right now, and that's what I was going to do for the next few weeks.

GEORGE   Oh, I understand that. As a matter of fact, I was doing the same thing. I just didn't want to leave you with the image of some retarded romantic walking around town with your number and a handful of dimes.

JENNIE   Knowing that, I will sleep better . . . It was very nice talking to you, George. Goodbye.
   (She hangs up. He hangs up. She turns and goes into the kitchen. He thinks a moment, then looks at the paper and dials again. The phone rings in her apartment. She comes out of the kitchen, a little annoyed, and answers it) Hello?

GEORGE   This is the charming call.

JENNIE   I think I have a problem on my hands.

GEORGE   You don't. I promise. This is definitely our last conversation.

JENNIE   Then why did you call back?

GEORGE   I couldn't resist saying, "This is the charming call" . . . Seriously, I'm sorry if I intruded on your privacy. I know very much how you feel. And I liked the sound of your voice, and I also wanted to say, "I hope you get your head together in good health." This is now the end of the charming call. Goodbye.

(He hangs up. Caught off-guard, she looks at the phone, then hangs up. His call stops her halfway to her kitchen)

JENNIE *(Returns to the phone)* Hello?
(A laugh bubbles out of her)

GEORGE I was just trying to place your voice. California girl, right? U.C.L.A.?

JENNIE Born in Cleveland and I went to Bennington in Vermont.

GEORGE How about that? I was *so* close.

JENNIE That's where I've just come from.

GEORGE Bennington?

JENNIE Cleveland. I was visiting family.

GEORGE Aha.

JENNIE Aha what?

GEORGE Just aha. Acknowledgment. Comprehension. I understand.

JENNIE Oh. Well, aha to you, too.

GEORGE Leo told me what you did but I didn't pay any attention.

JENNIE Why not?

GEORGE His previous social arrangements for me all ended like the *Andrea Doria*.

JENNIE And yet here you are calling me.

GEORGE   Only by mistake.

JENNIE   No, no. The first call was a mistake, and the second one was a call back explaining the mistake. The charming call was yours.

GEORGE   That's true. You have a very good mind, Jennie Malone. Now you see why you got the charming call.

JENNIE   You're a writer, that's for sure. I took English Lit. This is what they call "repartee," isn't it?

GEORGE   No. This is what they call "amusing telephone conversation under duress" . . . So what is it you do?

JENNIE   I'm an actress. *(He doesn't respond)* No "aha"?

GEORGE   Leo didn't tell me you were an actress.

JENNIE   I'm sorry. Wrong career?

GEORGE   No. No. Actresses can be, uh, very nice.

JENNIE   Well, that's an overstatement but I appreciate your open-mindedness.

GEORGE   Wait a minute, I'm now extricating my mouth from my foot . . . There, that's better. So you're an actress and I'm a writer. I'm also a widower.

JENNIE   Yes. Faye told me.

GEORGE   Faye?

JENNIE Faye Medwick. She's the one pushing from my side.

GEORGE Leo is getting up a brochure on me. We'll send you one when they come in . . . I understand you're recently divorced?

JENNIE Yes . . . How deeply do you intend going into this?

GEORGE Sorry. Occupational hazard. I pry incessantly.

JENNIE That's okay. I scrutinize.

GEORGE Well, prying is second cousin to scrutiny.

JENNIE Wouldn't you know it? It turns out we're related.

GEORGE I don't know if you've noticed but we also talk in the same rhythm.

JENNIE Hmmm.

GEORGE Hmmm? What is "hmmm"?

JENNIE It's second cousin to aha! . . . You're a very interesting telephone person, Mr. Schneider. However, I have literally just walked in the door, and I haven't eaten since breakfast. It was really nice talking to you. Goodbye. (She hangs up, waits right there expectantly) He hurriedly dials. Her phone rings; she picks it up) As you were saying?

GEORGE Listen, uh, can I be practical for a second?

JENNIE   For a second? Yes.

GEORGE   They're not going to let up, you know.

JENNIE   Who?

GEORGE   The Pushers. Leo and Faye. They will persist and push and prod and leave telephone numbers under books until eventually we have that inevitable date.

JENNIE   Nothing is inevitable. Dates are man-made.

GEORGE   Whatever... The point is, I assume you have an active career. I'm a very busy man who needs quiet and few distractions. So let me propose, in the interest of moving on with our lives, that we get this meeting over with just as soon as possible.

JENNIE   Surely you jest.

GEORGE   I'm not asking for a date. Blind dates are the nation's third leading cause of skin rash.

JENNIE   Then what are you suggesting?

GEORGE   Just hear me out. What if we were to meet for just five minutes? We could say hello, look each other over, part company and tell Leo and Faye that they have fulfilled their noble mission in life.

JENNIE   That's very funny.

GEORGE   And yet I hear no laughter.

JENNIE   Because it's not *funny* funny. It's stupid funny.

GEORGE   You think it's smart to suffer an entire evening rather than a quick five-minute "hello and goodbye"?

JENNIE   Because it's demeaning. It's like shopping. And I don't like being shopped.

GEORGE   Do you prefer window-shopping? I could stand across the street, look up and wave.

JENNIE   Am I talking to a serious person?

GEORGE   My friends tell me I have a certain charm. It's like gold, though. You have to pan for it.

JENNIE   And what if during these five minutes we took a liking to each other?

GEORGE   Then we take a shot at six minutes.

JENNIE   *But* if you take a fancy to me and I don't to you—or, God forbid, vice versa—what then?

GEORGE   It's a new system. We don't have all the bugs out yet.

JENNIE   I can't believe this conversation.

GEORGE   Look, if five minutes is too exhausting, we could have two-and-a-half-minute halves with an intermission.

JENNIE   Why am I intrigued by this? . . . When would you like this momentous occasion to take place?

GEORGE   How about right now?

JENNIE   Right now? That's crazy.

GEORGE   You mean, not possible?

JENNIE   Oh, it's possible. It's just crazy.

GEORGE   Why not? I'm having trouble working anyway. And next week could be too late. Mrs. Jurgens
and I could be a hot item.

JENNIE   But I just got off a plane. I look terrible.

GEORGE   So do I, and I got off one two months ago.
And besides, fixing yourself up is illegal. That's a
date. This is just a quick look for Leo and Faye.

JENNIE   For Leo and Faye, huh? . . . Oh, what the hell,
let's give it a shot.

GEORGE   Hey, terrific! Where would you like to meet?

JENNIE   How does Paris strike you?

GEORGE   Outside is no good. Then it gets down to
who says goodbye and who leaves first. Very messy
. . . How about your place?

JENNIE   That's out of the question.

GEORGE   Why?

JENNIE   I don't *know* why . . . 386 East Eighty-fourth
Street, apartment 12F.

GEORGE   Got it.

JENNIE   Write it down. You have a bad history with
numbers.

GEORGE   I'll be there in eight minutes.

JENNIE   And you don't think this is a bizarre thing to do?

GEORGE   It is the weirdest thing I've ever come up with. But we may be blazing the trail for millions of others.

JENNIE   And neither of us will be disappointed if we're disappointed, right?

GEORGE   Please. Let's not build down our hopes too much. See you. Goodbye.

JENNIE   Goodbye.
        (He hangs up. She hangs up)

GEORGE   Smart! Smart move, George!

JENNIE   Dumb! You're a dumb lady, Jennie Malone!
        (They head in opposite directions)

SCENE 6

Her apartment. Twenty minutes later. The phone rings.
JENNIE *comes out of the bedroom. She has taken off her blouse*
and is buttoning a new one. She goes to the phone quickly.

JENNIE *(Into the phone)* Hello? . . . Faye, I can't talk to
you now . . . He's on his way over . . . George
Schneider . . . Yes, *your* George Schneider . . . It's
not a date. It's a look! He looks at me and I look at
him and then you don't bother us anymore . . . Faye,
I can't talk to you now. I'll call you back when he
leaves in five minutes . . . Because that's all it takes.
(The doorbell rings) Dammit, he's here . . . I hate you.
Goodbye.
 (She hangs up, tucks her blouse into her skirt, looks in
 the mirror, does a last-minute brush job, then goes to
 the door. She takes in a deep breath, and then opens
 it. GEORGE *stands there, arm extended, leaning*
 against the doorframe. They look at each other . . .
 Finally he smiles and nods his head)

GEORGE Yeah! Okayyyyyy!

JENNIE Is that a review?

GEORGE No. Just a response . . . Hello.

JENNIE *(Smiles)* Hello.
 (They are both suddenly very embarrassed and don't

quite know what to say or how to handle this situation)

GEORGE *(Good-naturedly)* This was a dumb idea, wasn't it?

JENNIE Extremely.

GEORGE *(Nods in agreement)* I think I've put undue pressure on these next five minutes.

JENNIE You could cut it with a knife.

GEORGE I think if I came in, it would lessen the tension.

JENNIE Oh, I'm sorry. Please, yes.
(He steps in. She closes the door behind her)

GEORGE *(Looks around the room and nods)* Aha!

JENNIE Does that mean you comprehend my apartment?

GEORGE No. It means I like it. "Aha" can be used in many situations, this being one of them.

JENNIE Can I get you anything to drink?

GEORGE No, thanks. I don't drink.

JENNIE Oh, neither do I.
(There is an awkward pause)

GEORGE Although I'd love a glass of white wine.

JENNIE So would I. *(She goes to the kitchen)* Please, sit down.

GEORGE Thank you. *(But he doesn't. He wanders around the room looking at things. She brings in an opened bottle of white wine in an ice bucket set on a tray with two glasses. He spots a framed photograph of a football player in action)* Is it all right if I pry?

JENNIE Sure.

GEORGE You can scrutinize later. *(He examines the picture)* Oh, are you a football fan?

JENNIE That's my ex-husband. He was a wide receiver for the New York Giants.

GEORGE No kidding! What's his name?

JENNIE Gus Hendricks.

GEORGE *(Looks at picture again)* Gus Hendricks? . . . Funny, I can't remember him. How wide a receiver was he?

JENNIE He was cut the beginning of his second year. Bad hands, I think they call it. Couldn't hold on to the football.

GEORGE Well, some coaches are very demanding. What does he do now?

JENNIE Well, he was in mutual funds, he was in the saloon business, he was in broadcasting, he was in sports promotion—

GEORGE Very ambitious.

JENNIE He did all those in three months. He has some problems to work out.

(She pours the two glasses of wine)

GEORGE Who doesn't?

JENNIE True enough.
(She hands him a glass)

GEORGE Thank you.

JENNIE Here's to working out problems.
(They both drink. He looks at her)

GEORGE Leo was right. You're very attractive.

JENNIE Thank you.

GEORGE I'm curious. You don't have to answer this
. . . How was *I* described?

JENNIE "Not gorgeous, but an intelligent face."

GEORGE *(Smiles)* That's true. I have. You can ask my
face anything. (JENNIE *sits.* GEORGE *is still standing*)
No matter how old or experienced you are, the process never seems to get any easier, does it?

JENNIE What process?

GEORGE Mating.

JENNIE *Mating?* My God, is *that* what we're doing?

GEORGE *(Sits next to her on the sofa)* Haven't you noticed? First thing I did as I passed you, I inhaled.
Got a little whiff of your fragrance. In our particular species, the sense of smell is a determining factor
in sexual attraction.

43

JENNIE   This is just a guess. Do you write for *Field and Stream?*

GEORGE   *(Laughs)*   Please, give me a break, will you? I haven't done this in fourteen years. If you're patient, I get interesting with a little kindness.

JENNIE   You're not uninteresting now.

GEORGE   I'll tell you the truth. You're not the first girl Leo's introduced me to. There were three others ... All ranked with such disasters as the *Hindenburg* and Pearl Harbor.

JENNIE   *Now* I see. That's when the Five-Minute Plan was born.

GEORGE   Necessity is the Mother of Calamity.

JENNIE   Tell me about them.

GEORGE   Oh, they defy description.

JENNIE   Please. Defy it.

GEORGE   All right. Let's see. First there was Bambi. Her name tells you everything.

JENNIE   I got the picture.

GEORGE   Then there was Vilma. A dynamite girl.

JENNIE   Really?

GEORGE   Spent three years in a Turkish prison for carrying dynamite ... Need I go on?

JENNIE   No, I think I've had enough.

GEORGE Since then I've decided to take everything Leo says with a grain of panic . . . And now I feel rather foolish because I was very flippant with you on the phone, and now I find myself with an attractive, intelligent and what appears to be a very nice girl.

JENNIE You won't get a fight from me on that.

GEORGE With an appealing sense of adventure.

JENNIE You think so?

GEORGE It's your five minutes, too.

JENNIE I was wondering why I said yes. I think it's because I really enjoyed talking to you on the phone. You're very bright, and I found I had to keep on my toes to keep up with you.

GEORGE Oh. And is that unusual?

JENNIE I haven't been off my heels in years . . . What kind of books do you write?

GEORGE Ah, we're moving into heavy territory. What kind of books do I write? For a living, I write spy novels. For posterity, I write good novels. I make a good living, but my posterity had a bad year.

JENNIE Name some books.

GEORGE From column A or column B?

JENNIE Both.

GEORGE   Well, the spy novels I write under the name of Kenneth Blakely Hyphen Hill.

JENNIE   Hyphen Hill?

GEORGE   You don't say the hyphen. You just put it in.

JENNIE   Oh, God, yes. Of course. I've seen it. Drugstores, airports . . .

GEORGE   Unfortunately, not libraries.

JENNIE   Who picked the name?

GEORGE   My wife. You see, my publisher said spy novels sell better when they sound like they were written in England. We spent our honeymoon in London, and we stayed at the Blakely Hotel, and it was on a hill and the hall porter's name was Kenneth . . . If we had money in those days, my name might have been Kenneth Savoy Grill.

JENNIE   And from column B?

GEORGE   I only had two published. They were a modest failure. That means "Bring us more but not too soon."

JENNIE   I'd like to read them someday.

GEORGE   I'll send you a couple of cartons of them. *(They both sip their wine. He looks around, then back at her)* I'm forty-two years old.

JENNIE   Today?

GEORGE   No. In general.

46

JENNIE   Oh. Is that statement of some historic importance?

GEORGE   No. I just wanted you to know, because you
look to be about twenty-four and right now I feel
like a rather inept seventeen, and I didn't want you
to think I was too young for you.

JENNIE   I'm thirty-two.
*(They look at each other. It's the first time their gaze
really holds)*

GEORGE   Well. That was very nice wasn't it? I mean,
looking at each other like that.

JENNIE   I wasn't scrutinizing.

GEORGE   That's okay, I wasn't prying.

JENNIE   My hunch is that you're a very interesting
man, George.

GEORGE   Well, my advice is—play your hunches.

JENNIE   Can I get you some more, wine?

GEORGE   No thanks. I think I'd better be going.

JENNIE   *Oh? . . .* Okay.
(They rise)

GEORGE   Not that I wouldn't like to stay.

JENNIE   Not that you're not welcome, but I understand.

GEORGE   I think we've hit it off very well, if you've
noticed.

JENNIE I've noticed.

GEORGE Therefore, I would like to make a regulation date. Seven to twelve, your basic normal hours.

JENNIE Aha! With grown-up clothes and make-up?

GEORGE Bath, shower—everything.

JENNIE Sounds good. Let's make it.

GEORGE You mean now?

JENNIE Would you rather go home and do it on the phone?

GEORGE No, no. Dangerous. I could get the wrong number and wind up with Mrs. Jurgens . . . Let's see, what is this?

JENNIE Tuesday.

GEORGE How about Wednesday?

JENNIE Wednesday works out well.

GEORGE You could play hard to get and make it Thursday.

JENNIE No. Let's stick with Wednesday and I'll keep you waiting half an hour.

GEORGE *(At the door)* Fair enough. This was nice. I'm very glad we met, Jennie.

48

JENNIE So am I, George.

GEORGE I can't believe you're from the same man
who gave us Bambi and Vilma.
*(He goes. She closes the door, smiles and heads for her
bedroom. The lights fade)*

Her apartment. It is a week later, about 6:30 P.M. FAYE
*is staring out the window through binoculars, a cigarette in
her hand. She is looking a little glum.*

FAYE   She's putting on weight.

JENNIE *(Offstage)*   Who?

FAYE   Lupe, across the street. Sagging a little, too.
Another six pounds, she'll start pulling down her
shades.

JENNIE *(Offstage)*   You sound terrible. Is anything
wrong?

FAYE   We're not going away for Easter. Sidney's ear
infection still hasn't cleared up. He's lost his sense
of balance. He keeps rolling away from me in bed.
It's a very sad state of affairs when things are worse
at home than they are on the soap . . . They tell me
you're coming back to work on Monday.

JENNIE *(Offstage)*   Maybe. We'll see.

FAYE   You haven't given me a straight answer in a
week. What's all the mystery about? . . . Can I come
in now? Jennie? I'm alone enough at nights.

JENNIE *(Offstage)*   Give me ten more seconds.

FAYE   Four nights in one week, he's got to be someone special. Who is he, Jennie? Have I met him? Oh, God, I hate it when I'm left out of things! (JENNIE *comes out, shows off her new backless dress*) It's gorgeous. I love everything but the price tag.
   (They remove it)

JENNIE   Oh, damn, I'm a basket case. I haven't worried about looking good for someone in such a long time.

FAYE   What is going on, my angel?

JENNIE   I don't know. I've been on a six-day high and I've had nothing stronger than a Diet Pepsi.

FAYE   My God, it's George Schneider, isn't it? (JENNIE *nods*) Why didn't you tell me?

JENNIE   I was afraid to.

FAYE   Why?

JENNIE   Because after six days I think I'm nuts about him, and I was afraid if I told anyone they'd have me put in the Home for the Over-Emotional. Come on, I'm going to be late.

FAYE *(Going into the corridor)*   Well, tell me about him. What's he like?

JENNIE   Well, he's everything you've always wanted...
   (She closes the door, and they are gone)

His apartment, later that night.

JENNIE *(Outside his door)* Don't worry, I paid for the cab. *(She opens the door)* Where are the lights, George?

GEORGE *(In the corridor)* I don't want you to look at me.

JENNIE George, where are the lights?
(She finds them, turns them on)

GEORGE *(Entering, puts his hand to his eyes)* Oh, God, that hurts.

JENNIE Do you want to lie down, George?

GEORGE I'm so embarrassed. Just let me sit a few minutes. I'll be all right.

JENNIE Just keep taking deep breaths.

GEORGE *(Dizzy, sitting on the sofa)* That's the closest I've ever come to passing out.

JENNIE Loosen your collar. I'll take your shoes off.
(She kneels, starts to untie his laces as he loosens his tie and wipes his brow)

GEORGE First I thought it was the wine. Then I thought it was the fish. Then I figured it was the bill.

JENNIE   You don't know where they get the fish from anymore. *(She has his shoes off, massages his feet)* You read about tankers breaking up every day, oil spilling all over. For all we know, we just ate a gallon of Texaco.

GEORGE   Ohh. Ohh. Careful.

JENNIE   What?

GEORGE   I have very sensitive feet.

JENNIE   I'm sorry.

GEORGE   That's the weakest part of my system. Even baby powder hurts.

JENNIE   You're perspiring all over. Let me get you a cold towel.
    (She gets up, looks around, goes to the kitchen)

GEORGE   You mean my feet were sweaty? Oh, God! Is it over between us, Jennie?

JENNIE *(Coming back in with a wet cloth)*   Oh, shut up. I've rubbed sweaty feet before.

GEORGE   You have? You've really been around, haven't you? . . . I don't want you to think this is a regular thing, passing out on dates. I mean, I played varsity football at Hofstra.

JENNIE   I faint all the time. It's the only thing that relaxes me.
    (She puts the cloth on his forehead)

53

GEORGE Jesus! You paid for the taxi. How humiliating! I don't want to live anymore.

JENNIE You're not taking in enough air.
(She starts to unbuckle his belt and the top button of his pants)

GEORGE Hey! What are you doing?

JENNIE Oh, stop. I'm just unbuttoning your pants.

GEORGE Please! No premarital unbuckling! I'm all right, Jennie, really.

JENNIE *(She kneels down beside him)* You look about twelve years old right now.

GEORGE Seventeen last week, twelve this week—I'll be back in the womb by the end of the month. *(She kisses the back of his hand, then caresses it with her cheek. He touches her hair with his other hand)* You are the sweetest girl.

JENNIE *(Looks up at his face, smiles)* Thank you.
(He leans over and kisses her gently on the mouth)

GEORGE I can't believe it's just a week. I feel like we're into our fourth year or something.

JENNIE Have you felt that, too? As though it's not a new relationship at all. I feel like we're picking up in the middle somewhere . . . of something that started a long, long time ago.

GEORGE That's exactly how it was when I walked in your door that night last week. I didn't say to my-

54

self, "Oh, how pretty. How interesting. I wonder what she's like." I said, "Of course. It's Jennie. I know her. I never met her but I know her. How terrific to find her again."

JENNIE It's nice bumping into you again for the first time, George. *(They smile and kiss again. She looks up at him. He seems to have a pained expression on his face)* What is it? . . . Is it the pain again? *(He shakes his head "no," then turns away to hide the tears. He takes out a handkerchief to wipe his eyes)* George! Oh, George, sweetheart, what? Tell me.
    (She cradles his head in her arms as he tries to fight back his emotions)

GEORGE I don't know, Jennie.

JENNIE It's all right . . . Whatever you're feeling, it's all right.

GEORGE I keep trying to push Barbara out of my mind . . . I can't do it. I've tried, Jennie.

JENNIE I know.

GEORGE I don't really want to. I'm so afraid of losing her forever.

JENNIE I understand and it's all right.

GEORGE I know I'll never stop loving Barbara, but I feel so good about you . . . and I can't get the two things together in my mind.

JENNIE It all happened so fast, George. You expect so much of yourself so soon.

GEORGE   On the way over in the cab tonight, I'm yelling at the cab driver, "Can't you get there faster?" . . . And then some nights I wake up saying, "I'm never going to see Barbara again and I hope to God it's just a dream."

JENNIE   I love you, George . . . I want you to know that.

GEORGE   Give me a little time, Jennie. Stay next to me. Be with me. Just give me the time to tell you how happy you make me feel.

JENNIE   I'm not going anywhere, George. You can't lose me. I know a good thing when I see it.

GEORGE   *(Managing a smile)*   Jeez! I thought I had food poisoning and it's just a mild case of ecstasy.

JENNIE   *(Embraces him)*   I just want you to be happy. I want you to have room for all your feelings. I'll share whatever you want to share with me. I'm very strong, George. I can work a sixteen-hour day on a baloney sandwich and a milk shake. I have enough for both of us. Use it, George. Please. Use me . . .

GEORGE   *(Wipes his eyes, puts the hanky down)*   Really? Would you knit me a camel's-hair overcoat?

JENNIE   With or without humps? *(Touches his hand)* Why did it scare you so, George? We were sitting there touching hands, and you suddenly broke into a cold sweat.

GEORGE   Because it's not supposed to happen twice in your life.

JENNIE   Who said so?

GEORGE   Don't ask intelligent questions. You're talking to a man who just swooned into his butter plate. *(He rises)* Come on. I'll show you the house that Kenneth Blakely-Hill built.

JENNIE   And don't forget to give me those books tonight.

GEORGE   They're four ninety-five each, but we can talk business later. *(Puts his arm around her waist)* Now, then . . . This is the living room. That's the hallway that leads to the bedroom. And this is the rug that lies on the floor that covers the wood of the house that Kenneth Hyphen built.

JENNIE   I want to see everything.

GEORGE   Shall we start with the bedroom?

JENNIE   Okay.

GEORGE   If we start with the bedroom, we may *end* with the bedroom.

JENNIE   Endings are just beginnings backwards.

GEORGE   It's going to be one of those fortune cookie romances, huh? Okay, my dear . . . *(They head toward the bedroom)* Trust me.

JENNIE   I do.

GEORGE   Sure. I pass out at fish. What have *you* got to be afraid of?

(They enter the bedroom as the lights fade)

His apartment. It is three days later, mid-afternoon. LEO
paces in GEORGE*'s living room, takes some Valium from his
attaché case and swallows one with club soda.*

LEO   George, will you let somebody else in New York
use the phone?

GEORGE   *(Enters from the bedroom, wearing a sweater over
an open-necked shirt)*   I'm sorry, Leo. It was an important call. I had to take it.

LEO   Are you all right?

GEORGE   I'm wonderful! I'm terrific! I haven't felt this
good in such a long time . . . Listen, Leo, I'm glad
you dropped by.

LEO   You look tired. You don't have good color in
your face.

GEORGE   I'll have a painter come in Tuesday, he'll
show me some swatches. Leo, will you stop worry-
ing about me? I want to talk to you.

LEO   I called you one o'clock in the morning last
night, you weren't in.

GEORGE   I'm glad I wasn't. Why did you call me at one
o'clock in the morning?

LEO   I couldn't sleep. I wanted to talk to you.

GEORGE *(Impatient)* Leo! I am *fine*! Everything is *wonderful*!

LEO I wanted to talk about *me* . . . I'm in trouble, George.

GEORGE What?

LEO *(Nods)* Marilyn wants to leave me.

GEORGE *(Looks at him)* Oh, come on.

LEO What is that, a joke? My wife wants to leave me.

GEORGE Why?

LEO She's got a list. Ask her, she'll show it to you . . . She doesn't like my lifestyle, she doesn't like the hours I keep, my business, my friends, my indifference, my attitude, my coldness—and our marriage. Otherwise we're in good shape. Christ! I said to her, "Marilyn, show me a press agent who comes home at six o'clock and I'll show you a man who can't get Jimmy Carter's name in the newspapers." I'm in the theater. Life begins at eight o'clock. The world isn't just matinees.

GEORGE She's not going to leave you, Leo. This has been going on for years.

LEO I took on two extra shows this season. The money was good, we needed it. I can't tell what the future is. I've got to make it *now*! I've got two kids. I could be dead tomorrow.

GEORGE *(Nods)* That's possible. I guess she just wants to enjoy you while you're still alive.

LEO *(Referring to* GEORGE's *wife)* I'm sorry, George.

GEORGE Oh, come on, Leo. I know how you feel. You'll work it out. You always have.

LEO Not this time . . . She's leaving me the morning after *Pinocchio*.

GEORGE *Pinocchio?* What's that?

LEO Tina is doing *Pinocchio* at school. Marilyn doesn't want to upset her until it's over. The kid isn't even playing the lead. She's a herring that gets swallowed by the whale.

GEORGE When is the show?

LEO The show is Thursday night. The only chance I have to keep her is if the play runs four years! I don't know what the hell I'm holding on to, anyway. I swear to God, I'll never get married again. You spend half your married life fighting to get back the feeling you had just before you got married.

GEORGE Come on, Leo. You've got a good marriage— I *know*.

LEO Really? I'll invite you to sleep in our bedroom one night, you can listen. I'll tell you, George. The trouble with marriage is that it's relentless. Every morning when you wake up, it's still there. If I could just get a leave of absence every once in a while. A two-week leave of absence. I used to get them all the time in the Army, and I always came back . . . I don't know. I think it was different for you and Barbara. I'll tell you the truth, I always thought the two of you were a little crazy. But that's what made it work for you. You had a real bond of lunacy between you . . . Marilyn has no craziness. No fantasies. No uncharted territories to explore. I'm sitting there with maps for places in my mind I've never been, and she won't even pack an overnight bag. In eleven years she never once let me make love to her with the lights on. I said to her, "Marilyn, come on, trust me, I won't tell anybody." So we stop growing, stop changing. And we stagnate . . . in our comfortable little house in the country . . . Oh, well, another thirty, thirty-five years and it'll be over, right? *(He sits back)* All right, I've told someone. I feel better . . . Now, what the hell is it you feel so wonderful about?

GEORGE *(Smiles)* You're an interesting man, Leo. Someday I'll have to get to know you . . . In the meantime there's this girl I've met—

LEO You've gone out with her? You like her?

GEORGE I like her, Leo. She's extraordinary.

LEO *(Pleased)* Isn't that wonderful! You see, I knew you'd like her. I only spoke to her for ten minutes, but I saw she had a vitality, a sparkle about her—I knew she would interest you.

GEORGE She more than interests me, Leo. I'm crazy about her.

LEO Listen, I don't blame you. If I wasn't married, I'd have beaten you to the punch. Isn't that terrific! Terrific! Well, I knew once you left yourself open, you'd start to meet some women you can relate to—

GEORGE I'm in love with her, Leo—I mean, crazy in love with her.

LEO Well, we'll see. The point is, you enjoy being with her and that's very important for you at this time.

GEORGE Leo, you don't hear what I'm saying . . . I'm going to marry her.

LEO Look, it's possible. *I* hope so. She seems very sweet. Very bright. Faye tells me there isn't a person who ever met her who doesn't like her. She could be wonderful for you. When things calm down, when you get to be your old self again, I would *love* to see it happen.

GEORGE We're getting married on Monday.
     (LEO *looks at him*)

LEO Monday's a terrific day to get married. You miss the weekend traffic. Seriously, George, I'm glad you like the girl.

GEORGE We took the blood test. I got the license. It's Monday morning, ten o'clock, Judge Ira Markowitz's chambers. I'd like you and Marilyn to be there.

LEO   To be where?

GEORGE *(Annoyed)*   Come on, Leo, you heard me. Jennie and I are getting married on Monday morning.

LEO   Wait a minute, wait a minute, back up! Play that again. What are you telling me? You mean on Monday morning you're marrying a girl I met for twelve seconds in a restaurant?

GEORGE   I'm marrying Jennie! *Jennie Malone!*

LEO   Oh, good. You know both names. So you must have had a chance to talk to her.

GEORGE   I've lived with her twenty hours a day for the last two weeks, and I know everything I want to know about her.

LEO   Two weeks? You've known her two weeks? I eat eggs that are *boiled* for two weeks—what the hell is *two* weeks?

GEORGE   Wait a minute. What happened to "how interesting she is"? What happened to her vitality, her sparkle?

LEO   Can't you wait to see if she's still sparkling in six months?

GEORGE   Six days, six months—what the hell difference does it make? I only knew Barbara eight weeks, and the marriage lasted twelve years.

LEO George, you're vulnerable now. You're in no shape to make a decision like this.

GEORGE Wait a minute. You know me, Leo. I'm not self-destructive. I wouldn't do something to hurt me *and* Jennie just to satisfy a whim. I love her. I want to be with her. I want to make this commitment.

LEO It's my fault, George. I never should have introduced you to Bambi. After Bambi you were ready for anything.

GEORGE Leo, it was the same thing when I met Barbara. I could have married her after the third date. I knew then she was the most special girl in the world. Well, it's twelve years later and Barbara is gone. And suddenly, miraculously, this incredible person comes into my life—a sensitive, intelligent, warm, absolutely terrific human being. I don't know. Maybe it *is* crazy. You always said I was. But I'm miserable every minute I'm away from her, and she feels the same way. I think marrying her is a Class-A idea, Leo.

LEO Okay, okay. But what is she—Cinderella? She's leaving at twelve o'clock? Wait! You'd wait six weeks for a dentist appointment, and that's with *pain* in your mouth.

GEORGE Have dinner with us tonight. You and Marilyn.

LEO I really don't think a couple breaking up is the best company for a couple starting out.

GEORGE   Call Marilyn. Tell her. Maybe being around us will give you both a chance to work things out.

LEO *(Annoyed)*   Why can't you accept the fact that Marilyn and I are separating?

GEORGE   Why can't you accept the fact that Jennie and I are getting married?

LEO   Because my separation makes sense. Your getting married is crazy!

GEORGE   Have it your own way. But I would still like you both to be there on Monday.

LEO   George, you've always been a lot smarter than me in a lot of ways. You have the talent and the discipline I've always admired. I'm very proud of you. But once in a while I've steered you straight, and I don't think you've ever regretted it . . . Wait a couple of months. Let her move in here with you. Is she against that? She's not a Mormon or anything, is she?

GEORGE   What's the point of delaying what's inevitable? She'll wait if I ask her.

LEO   Ask her.

GEORGE   She'll move in if I ask her.

LEO   Ask her. Please, George, ask her.

GEORGE   Monday morning, Criminal Courts building. I'm wearing a blue suit.

LEO   Wait a month. Wait a month for *me*.

66

GEORGE I'm not marrying *you*!

LEO Wait a month for me, and I'll wait a month for you. I'll try to work things out with Marilyn. I'll keep us together somehow, for a month, if you and Jennie will do the same for me.

GEORGE Leo, we're not trading baseball cards now. This is my life, that's your marriage. Save it for you and Marilyn, not for me.

LEO George, I realize I'm not the best marriage counselor you could go to—the toll-taker in the Lincoln Tunnel is more qualified than me—all I'm saying is take the time to catch your breath. Sleep on it. Take twelve Valiums and wake up in a month.

GEORGE We're wasting a lot of time, you know that, Leo? This conversation used up my entire engagement period.

LEO Would you mind if I talked to her?

GEORGE Jennie?

LEO Yes. Would you mind if I met with her, alone, and told her how I feel about all this?

GEORGE Yes, I certainly would. She doesn't need an interview to get into this family.

LEO Are you afraid she might agree with me?

GEORGE Leo, I was always bigger than you . . . and you always beat up the kids who picked on me. What Pop didn't do for me, you did. I was the only kid on the block who had to buy *two* Father's Day presents...All right. Look, you want to protect me? Go ahead. You want to talk to Jennie, talk to her. But I promise you—a half-hour with her and you'll come back wondering why I'm waiting so long.

LEO   Thank you. I'll call Jennie tonight.

GEORGE   Would you like me to talk with Marilyn? I could wrap up the four of us in one night.

LEO   Listen, I could be wrong. I've been wrong before.

GEORGE   When?

LEO   I can't remember when, but I must have been ... *(Goes to the door)* I don't know what the hell I'm doing in publicity. I was born to be a Jewish mother.

  (He leaves. GEORGE *thinks a moment, then goes to the phone and dials. In* JENNIE*'s apartment the phone rings. She's been reading* Catch-22*)*

JENNIE   *(Answering the phone)*   Hello?

GEORGE   I love you. Do you love me?

JENNIE   Of course I do . . . Who is this?

GEORGE   You're going to get a call from my brother. He thinks we're crazy.

JENNIE   Of course we are. What else is new?

GEORGE   Jennie, I've been thinking...Let's call it off. Let's wait a month. Maybe a couple of months.

68

JENNIE   All right . . . Whatever you say.

GEORGE   And I'd like you to move in here with me.
Until we decide what to do.

JENNIE   I'll move in whenever you want.

GEORGE   I'm crazy about you.

JENNIE   I feel the same way.

GEORGE   Then forget what I said. It's still on for Monday morning.

JENNIE   I'll be there with my little bouquet!
(They hang up. JENNIE *looks thoughtful.* GEORGE'*s
gaze is drawn to a framed photo of Barbara)*
Curtain

Act Two

His apartment. It's the next afternoon. GEORGE *is stretched out on his sofa, the phone to his ear. He is in the midst of a difficult conversation.*

GEORGE Of course I am . . . Yes . . . An incredible girl . . . Mom, why would I marry her if I wasn't? . . . Her father sells insurance in Cleveland . . . Yes, he also lives there, that's why he works there. *(He holds the receiver aside and emits a deep sigh of exasperation. Then he puts the phone back to his ear)* . . . I just told you. Monday morning. In a judge's office . . . How can it be, Mom? How can it be a big wedding in a judge's office? . . . You'll meet her when you come up from Florida. *(Another deep sigh. The doorbell rings)* Hold it a second, Mom, the doorbell's ringing . . . No. *Mine!*
  (He shakes his head, puts down the phone, opens the door. JENNIE *stands there, beaming)*

JENNIE I'm so crazy about you, it's ridiculous. *(She throws her arms around him and kisses him)* You're the most perfect man who ever lived on the face of the earth.

GEORGE Jeez, if I hear that one more time today . . . What are you doing here?

JENNIE   I just had a physical, a facial and a dental. I don't want to get returned because of an imperfection. And I bought you a present.
(She takes a package from her purse and hands it to him)

GEORGE   What is it?

JENNIE   Open it. *(He does. It is two books bound in fine leather)* Two from column B. I bought them at Doubleday's. They had to order them from the publisher.

GEORGE   *(Overwhelmed)* You had them bound? In leather?

JENNIE   Guaranteed to last as long as Dickens and Twain.

GEORGE   I'm speechless. I'm so thrilled, I don't know what to say . . . I mean, the leather binding is beautiful—but to think I sold two more books! *(He hugs her)* Hey! I left my mother on the phone.

JENNIE   In Florida? I want to speak to her.

GEORGE   Mom? . . . The next voice you are about to hear is that of Jennie Malone, a girl who brings dignity and respect to the often maligned phrase, "future daughter-in-law"!

JENNIE   *(Into the phone)* Mrs. Schneider? . . . Hello . . . I'm very happy to meet you . . . Oh, how nice . . . Well, I am too . . . I hope you know you have a very special and wonderful son.

GEORGE   She knows, she knows.

JENNIE   No . . . No, it's not going to be a big wedding. It's going to be in a judge's office.

GEORGE   *(Into the phone extension)*   She drinks, Mom . . . And she's a jockey at Belmont.
   (He hangs up)

JENNIE   All right, I will . . . Yes . . . As soon as we get back from Barbados . . . God bless you, too.
   (JENNIE, *suddenly taken with tears, hands the phone to* GEORGE)

GEORGE   *(Into the phone)*   Mom, I'll be right with you. Hang on. Watch Merv Griffin. (He lays the phone down and embraces JENNIE) She can drive you completely nuts and then say something that just wipes you out.

JENNIE   Listen, I'll let you work. Don't be late tonight. I'm making spaghetti with fresh basil sauce.

GEORGE   Wait a minute. I bought you a present too. *(He goes to a drawer, opens it and takes out a ring box)* I was going to wait until after dinner, but I think I'm going to be eating a long time.
   (He hands it to her. She is excited, knowing full well what it probably is)

JENNIE *(Beside herself)*   Oh, George, George, what have you done?

GEORGE   It's a car.

JENNIE *(Taking out a small diamond ring)* Oh, George...

GEORGE It's no big deal. It's just a wholesale engagement ring.

JENNIE But we'll only be engaged for two more days.

GEORGE Well, what I paid, that's all it's going to last.

JENNIE This is too much emotion for me in one day. Come a half-hour late—I need more time to cry. *(And she rushes to the door, stops and goes back to the phone)* Hello, Mom, he gave me a ring.
(She runs out, and into her own apartment)

GEORGE *(Into the phone)* Mom? . . . No, she left . . . Thank you . . . Of course she knows about Barbara . . . Well, in *my* day we discuss things, Mom . . . What else am I doing? You mean besides getting married? . . . Well, I bought a new sports jacket . . . Gray . . . You can never have too much gray, Mom . . . *(Dimout)*

Her apartment. The doorbell rings. JENNIE *goes over to it. The lights come up on his apartment.* GEORGE, *having finished his long conversation with his mother, dials the phone, sitting up.* JENNIE *opens the door.* FAYE *stands there, her hair in curlers, covered with a scarf.*

JENNIE   I thought you were taping two shows today.

FAYE   We're on a lunch break. If I asked you for an enormous favor, would you say yes and not ask any questions?

JENNIE   Yes.

FAYE   How long are you keeping this apartment?
(*The phone rings*)

JENNIE   My lease is up in two months. Why?

FAYE   Would you let me have the key?
(JENNIE *looks at her. The phone rings again. She picks it up. It is* GEORGE)

JENNIE   Hello?

GEORGE   My mother said no. I'm awfully sorry.

JENNIE   I am too.

GEORGE   I think we could have made a go of it, but this is too great an obstacle.

77

JENNIE   Don't worry about it. I have other things to do.

GEORGE   She found someone else for me. But good news: You're invited to the reception.

JENNIE   So we can still see each other.

GEORGE   Certainly. We can chat over an hors d'oeuvre . . . I'm going to take a bath now. I know you like to follow my schedule.

JENNIE   I read it. It was in the *Times*.

GEORGE   Then there's no point in talking. Goodbye.

JENNIE   'Bye! (*They both hang up. He turns and heads for his bathroom as the lights go down on his apartment.* JENNIE *turns to* FAYE) Why do you want the key?

FAYE   You promised no questions.

JENNIE   That's before I knew the favor.

FAYE   Please.
    (JENNIE *sees that* FAYE *is serious. She crosses to her dresser, takes out a spare key, goes to* FAYE *and hands it to her*)

JENNIE   I don't want to know, Faye, but if it's something stupid, please don't do it.

FAYE   Then take the key back, because I don't know a smart way to have an affair.

JENNIE   Ohhh, Christ! What have you done?

FAYE   Everything but consummation. That's why I need the key.

JENNIE   When did all this happen?

FAYE   All what? So far it's only ten percent cocktail talk . . . But I'm leaning toward "happening."

JENNIE   I don't want to know who it is.

FAYE   It's a secret I'll keep to my grave.

JENNIE   Why won't you tell me?

FAYE   Because it's not important who it is. It's only important that I want to do it. Don't you understand, Jennie? If I don't have something like an affair, I'll scream.

JENNIE   Then scream!

FAYE   Well, I thought I'd try this first.

JENNIE   Listen, maybe you're right. You're a grown lady, you know what you're doing.

FAYE   The hell I do.

JENNIE   Then why are you doing it?

FAYE   You tell me. Why are you getting married to a man you've known two and a half weeks who was married to a woman he idolized for twelve years? Because yesterday was lousy and it seems right today. I'll worry about tomorrow the day after.

79

JENNIE "The Wit and Wisdom of Women in Trouble." Someday we'll collaborate on it . . . Is there anything I can do to help?

FAYE Just leave me a map of all quick exits from the apartment . . . I've got to get back to making America cry. *(Holding up the key)* Listen, I may never use this, but you're the best friend I ever had.

JENNIE When is this—*thing* going to take place?

FAYE Oh, not for a few days. I have to be hypnotized first.

(She exits. The phone rings; JENNIE *answers it)*

JENNIE Hello? . . . Hello, my angel . . . I thought you were taking a bath . . . Oh, you are! . . . No, I do *not* want to hear you blow bubbles . . . I do not want to hear your rubber duck. You're down to three years old, George, and sinking fast. *(The doorbell rings)* Oh, I think that's Leo . . . I'll see you for dinner . . . Well, I'm having spaghetti and you're having baby food. 'Bye!

(She hangs up and opens the door)

LEO Hello, Jennie.

JENNIE Leo—come on in. *(He enters)* I really enjoyed dinner the other night. Marilyn is a very sweet girl.

LEO Thank you. We'll have to have you out to the house when you two get settled.

JENNIE I'd love it . . . Would you like some coffee and stale cookies? I'm trying to clean out the kitchen.

LEO A few minutes. That's all I'm staying. I just wanted to state my case and leave.

JENNIE Oh? That sounds serious . . . All right. Please sit.

LEO *(Decides to stand)* This is none of my business, you know. I have no right coming up here.

JENNIE I think loving your brother is very much your business.

LEO I'm glad you feel that way. Because I do. The reason I wanted to talk to you, Jennie—and if I'm out of line here, tell me . . . the reason I came up here today . . . The foundation for my thoughts . . . The . . . the structure for my desire to . . . to delineate the . . . What the hell am I saying? The structure to delineate—what is that?

JENNIE You think George and I are going too fast.

LEO Exactly. Thank you! Christ! I thought that sentence would take me right into middle age.

JENNIE Two weeks *is* very fast.

LEO In some circles it's greased lightning . . . Be that as it may—and I hasten to add that I have never used expressions like "Be that as it may" or "I hasten to add"—but I'm having trouble. This is delicate territory, and I'm dealing with someone I care very much about.

JENNIE Leo, I told George I'd wait as long as he wanted. Two weeks, two months—I don't care how long. He said, "No. It's got to be Monday, the twenty-third. It's all arranged" . . . What is it you're afraid will happen, Leo?

LEO *(Takes a news clipping from his wallet)* I don't know . . . I'm not sure. Listen, I once did some work for an insurance company and they published these statistics—it was in every national magazine . . . *(Reads)* "The greatest loss that can happen to a man or woman, in terms of traumatic impact to the survivor, is the death of a spouse. The loss of a parent, a child, a job, a house—any catastrophe—is not deemed as devastating as the death of a husband or wife." In time, thank God and the laws of nature, most people work through it. But it needs the time . . . And I wouldn't want you and George to be hurt because that time was denied to him—to both of you.

JENNIE I see . . . Have you and George talked about this?

LEO I can't always read George's mind. He keeps so much bottled up. Maybe he spills it all out when he's alone—at the typewriter. I don't know.

JENNIE Can I ask you a question?

LEO What?

JENNIE What was it like when Barbara died?

LEO Ohhh . . . I don't think you want to go through that, Jennie.

JENNIE   No, I don't . . . But you just made it clear how important it is that I do. Tell me, Leo.

LEO *(Thinks, takes his time)*   All right . . . They were very close. I mean, as close as any couple I've ever seen. After ten years, they still held hands in a restaurant. I'm married eleven years and I don't pass the salt to my wife . . . When George first found out how ill Barbara was, he just refused to accept it. He knew it was serious, but there was no way she was not going to beat it. He just couldn't conceive of it. And Barbara never let on to a soul that anything was ever wrong. Her best friend, at the funeral, said to George, "I just didn't know" . . . She was beautiful, Jennie, in every way. And then in the last few months you could see she was beginning to slip. George would go out to dinner or a party and leave early, trying not to let on that anything was wrong —and especially not letting on to themselves . . . And then one morning George called me from the hospital, and he said very quietly and simply, "She's gone, Leo." And it surprised me because I thought when it was finally over, George would go to pieces. I mean, I expected a full crackup, and it worried me that he was so held together . . . I saw him as often as I could, called him all the time, and then suddenly I didn't hear from him for about five days. He didn't answer the phone. I called the building. They said they didn't see him go in or go out, and I got plenty scared. I went up there—they let me in with the passkey—and I found him in the bedroom sitting in front of the television set, with the picture on and no sound. He was in filthy pajamas, drenched in perspiration. There was a container of milk on the floor next to him that had gone sour. He must have dropped eight or nine pounds. And I said to him, "Hey, George, why don't you answer your phone? Are you okay?" And he said, "Fine. I'm fine, Leo." Then he reached over and touched my hand, and for the first time in a year and a half, the real tears started to flow. He cried for hours—through that whole night. I still couldn't get him to eat, so the next morning I got our doctor to come over, and he checked him into Mount Sinai. He was there for ten days. And he was in terrible shape. His greatest fear was that I was going to commit him someplace. When he came out, he stayed with me about a week. I couldn't even get him to take a walk. He had this panic, this fear he'd never make it back into the house. I finally got him to walk down to the corner, and he never let go of my arm for a second. We started across the street and he stopped and said, "No, it's too far. Take me back, Leo." A few weeks later he went into therapy. A really good doctor. He was there about a month, and then suddenly he decided he wasn't going back. He wouldn't explain why. I called the doctor and he explained to me that George was making a very determined effort not to get better. Because getting better meant he was ready to let go of Barbara, and there was no way he was going to let that happen. And then one day, bang, he took off for Europe. But not new places.

Only the ones he'd visited with Barbara before. When he came back he looked better, seemed more cheerful. So in my usual dumb, impulsive way, I figured he would want what I would want if I were in his place—companionship. Well, companionship to him and me, I found out, were two different things. But he has good instincts. He knows what's right for him. And God knows what I offered wasn't right . . . until the night I saw you sitting there with Faye and I said, "Oh yeah, that's for George." I swear to you, Jennie, you are the best thing that could happen to that man. I was just hoping it would happen a little later . . . I'm sorry. No matter how I say all this, it doesn't seem to come out right. But you wanted to hear it. I just felt I had an obligation to say it. I hope you understand that, Jennie.

JENNIE   I'm trying hard to.

LEO   In other words, I think the smart thing to do is wait . . . to get one thing over with before you start something new. Is it unfair of me to say that?

JENNIE   Maybe it was your timing that was wrong. It was the most detailed, descriptive, harrowing story any woman who's just about to get married ever heard.

LEO   I'm sorry. The bluntness comes from twenty-one years in the newspaper business.

JENNIE   Jesus God, what a thing to hear. I know you're concerned about your brother—maybe you should have given a little consideration to your future sister-in-law.

LEO   Jennie, please . . .

JENNIE   Forgive me. I'm sorry. But just let me get angry a second, because I think I deserve it.

LEO   I came here to talk, I didn't come here to fight.

JENNIE   No, maybe you're right, Leo. Maybe George really hasn't dealt with Barbara's death yet. And maybe I haven't asked enough questions. I can only deal with one thing at a time. Let me experience my happiness before I start dealing with the tragedies . . . Even if there were no Barbara to deal with, this is scary enough. And I'm goddamned petrified!

LEO   Well, you shouldn't be.

JENNIE   What do you mean, I shouldn't be? The thing I was most frightened to hear, you just sat there and told me.

LEO   That he loved her?

JENNIE   Yes!

LEO   That he was miserable when she died?

JENNIE   Yes! Yes! Of course I know it, but I don't want to hear it. Not now. Not today. My God, I'm moving into the woman's house Monday afternoon.

LEO   That's my point.

JENNIE   I'll wait as long as he wants. But it was his choice. He picked the date. And if that's not the sign of a man who wants to get healthy quickly, I don't know what is . . . Who picked me out as the stable one, Leo? I've just come from five years of analysis and a busted marriage. I couldn't believe how *lucky* I was when George came into my life . . . that he was going to make everything all right. And look at me —I'm so damned nervous everything might fall apart. It all feels like it's hanging by a string, and this sharp pair of scissors is coming towards me— snapping away.

LEO   Jennie, I swear to you, the only reason I brought it up at all is because I feel so responsible. I'm the one who made this match.

JENNIE   Well, let me put your mind at rest. There are powers even higher than matchmakers. I promise you, Leo, even if what we're doing is not right, I'll *make* it right.

LEO   *(After a pause)*   Okay, I'll buy that. *(Shakes her hand, smiles)* I'll see you Monday, kid.
    (He starts out)

JENNIE   Leo, do me a favor. Don't tell George what we talked about. Give us time to get to that ourselves.

LEO   I'm not even talking to George. I can't understand why he waited this long.
    (He opens door and leaves. She heads for the bedroom)

87

His apartment. Monday morning, about 9 A.M. GEORGE,
*dressed in a neat blue suit, is looking in the mirror at the
tissue covering a shaving cut on his jaw. He glances at his
watch; he is very nervous. He goes over to the phone and dials.*

GEORGE *(He listens for a minute, then speaks distinctly into
    the phone)* Doctor Ornstein . . . It's George
Schneider again . . . I don't think I can wait any
longer for you to get out of your session . . . I know
this is a weird message to be leaving on a recording
. . . I realize I should have called you sooner, but
frankly I was nervous about it . . . I'm getting married in about forty-five minutes and . . . She's a
wonderful girl and I know I'm doing the right thing
. . . I'll be at 273–4681, extension 1174, Judge Markowitz's chambers, in case you have to tell me something of the utmost importance, uh . . . Goodbye.
*(He hangs up and wipes his brow with a hanky, realizes
he's wearing slippers, runs toward the bedroom. The doorbell rings. He yells out)* It's open!
    (The door opens and LEO *comes in wearing a dark-
    blue suit and a white carnation in his lapel)*

LEO   I've been waiting downstairs fifteen minutes. I
watered my carnation three times. Are we getting
married today or not?

GEORGE *(Returning, shoes in hand)* I cut myself shaving. I can't stop bleeding. Was there any royalty in our family?

LEO Yeah. King Irving from White Plains. Come on. The cab is going to cost you more than the honeymoon.

GEORGE I slept twelve minutes—and I woke up *twice* during the twelve minutes.

LEO Let's go, George. The judge has a lot of murderers to convict today.

GEORGE *(Looks at him)* Who is she, Leo? I'm marrying a girl, I don't know who she is.

LEO Don't start with me! Don't give me trouble, George! You drove me and all your friends half-crazy and now suddenly you want information?

GEORGE I can't breathe. What a day I pick not to be able to breathe. What should I do, Leo?

LEO I'll buy you a balloon, you can suck on it! George, I've got to know. Are you calling this off? Because if you are, I can still catch a workout at the gym.

GEORGE *(Yells, annoyed)* Will you have a little goddamn compassion! I can't even get my ex-analyst on the phone. A lot *they* care. Fifty dollars an hour and all they do is protect you from doing neurotic things in *their* office. *(Gets a boxed carnation from the refrigerator)* Listen, if you're too busy, run along. Take the

89

cab. I don't want you at my wedding anyway. You're going to stand there and make funny faces. You do it all the time.

LEO   I did it at *my* wedding, never at yours. *(Sees* GEORGE *fumbling hopelessly with the cellophane wrapping of the carnation)* What are you doing? What is that, a forest fire? Hold it, hold it, *hold it!*
       (He pins the carnation on GEORGE*'s lapel)*

GEORGE   You never told me what you and Jennie talked about.

LEO   She wasn't home.

GEORGE   She told me I'm very lucky to have such a concerned brother.

LEO   And she told me *I'm* the one she really wants. She's just marrying you to make me jealous. Let's go, George. *(Starts to push* GEORGE *to the door)* If you're late, this judge fines you.
       *(*LEO *ushers* GEORGE *almost all the way out. He balks at the door)*

GEORGE   You were right, Leo. It's all too soon. I should have waited until eleven, eleven-thirty. Ten o'clock is too soon.

LEO   Will you *come on?*

GEORGE   I didn't even have breakfast!

LEO   I'll buy you an Egg McMuffin at McDonalds!
       *(*LEO *hustles* GEORGE *out)*

SCENE 4

Her apartment. FAYE *comes out of the bedroom in a sexy black negligee, wearing dark glasses, nervously smoking a cigarette, brushing her hair. She takes perfume from her bag, sprays it all over. Music plays on the radio. She goes to the door, looks out furtively.*

His apartment. A key opens the door. LEO *rushes to the phone, dials a number, takes the phone with him as he searches through desk drawers in a slight panic. The phone rings in* JENNIE's *apartment.* FAYE *is startled, looks at it. It rings again as* LEO *mutters, "Answer it, come on!" Finally she turns off the music and answers the phone.*

FAYE   Yes?

LEO   Faye?

FAYE   What number did you want, please?

LEO   It's all right, Faye. It's me, Leo.

FAYE   Leo who?

LEO   Faye, I haven't got time to play espionage! I can't meet you now. I've got to rush back out to the airport. George forgot the airline tickets and his traveler's checks, the limousine had a flat on the Long Island Expressway, and Jennie's got the heaves . . . Can we do it tomorrow?

FAYE No. Tomorrow's no good. Sidney and I are going to the marriage counselor.

LEO What time do you get through?

FAYE I'm going *there* so I don't have to come *here!*

LEO Cool it, cool it! Let's not get untracked before the train gets started—

FAYE Leo, please. Let's forget it. I can't go through with it.

LEO Why?

FAYE I was seen by two little girls in the elevator.

LEO Faye, please stop treating this like it's the Watergate break-in. You think we're the only ones doing this? What do you think they have lunch hours for? ... I've got to run. There are two people about to leave for their honeymoon who aren't talking to each other. I'll call you later.

FAYE No, Leo—

LEO I'm hungry for you ... hot, steaming, roasting, burning hungry with desire. *(Kissing and hissing sounds)* 'Bye. *(Hangs up, looks at his watch)* Oh, shit! *(He rushes out of the apartment.* FAYE *hangs up and sits there glumly)*

FAYE This is definitely my last affair.
(She goes into the bedroom. Dimout)

SCENE 5

His apartment. It is a week later, about 8 P.M. We hear the sound of thunder, then of rain. The door opens. GEORGE *enters, carrying straw bags and suitcases. He looks rather bedraggled.* JENNIE *follows him in, carrying suitcases and her shoulder bag, along with a large straw hat and bongo drums —bought in the tropics, no doubt. She drops them with a thud, then goes over to the sofa and falls into it, exhausted, her legs outstretched.*

GEORGE *picks up his mail, which was tied with a rubber band and left inside his door. He closes the door, and stands there going through the letters meticulously. Both are silent and there is some degree of tension between them.*

JENNIE *(Looks up at the ceiling, mournfully)* That was fun! Three days of rain and two days of diarrhea. We should have taken out honeymoon insurance.

GEORGE *(Without looking up)* Don't forget to put your watch back an hour.

JENNIE I don't want the hour. Let 'em keep it! ... Any mail for me?
(He opens and reads a letter)

GEORGE *(Looks at her)* You've only been *living* here thirty-eight seconds.

JENNIE Are you going to read your mail *now*?

93

GEORGE   It's from my publisher. He wants some revisions.

JENNIE   Again? You "revised" in Barbados . . . Is there anything soft to drink?

GEORGE   *(Testy)*   I think there's some beer. I could strain it if you like.

JENNIE   No, thanks. We have all the "strain" we can handle. *(She crosses to the fridge)* I read somewhere you can tell everything about a person by looking inside his refrigerator. *(She opens it)* Oh, God! Is this the man I married? Cold and empty, with a little yogurt?

GEORGE   I'll call the grocer in the morning and have him fill up my personality.

JENNIE   *(Takes out a half-empty bottle of Coke with no cap on it)*   You want to share a half a bottle of opened Coke? None of that annoying fizz to worry about. *(She takes a swig)*

GEORGE   *(Looks at her, not amused)*   How many glasses of wine did you have on the plane?

JENNIE   Two.

GEORGE   How many?

JENNIE   Four.

GEORGE   You had seven.

JENNIE   I had six.

GEORGE   And two at the airport. That's *eight*.

JENNIE   All right, it was eight. But it wasn't seven. Don't accuse me of having seven.

GEORGE   *(Gets up)*   You're tight, Jennie.
   (He picks up the suitcases and coats)

JENNIE   Ohhh, is that what's been bothering you all day, George? That I drank too much? I can't help it: I don't like flying. I asked you to hold my hand, but you wouldn't do it. So I drank some wine instead.

GEORGE   *(Starts for the bedroom with the bags)*   I *did* hold your hand. And while I was holding it, you drank my wine.
   (He goes into the bedroom)

JENNIE   All right, George. Get it all out. You're angry because I ate your macadamia nuts, too, aren't you? And your package of Trident chewing gum. And I read the *Time* magazine you bought *before* you. You're sore because I knew what happened to "People in the News" ahead of you.
   (She glances through the mail)

GEORGE   Don't mix up my mail, please.

JENNIE   *(Puts it back)*   *Pardonnez-moi.* I'll "revise" it later. *(He takes off his jacket. She tries to be more cheerful)* It's a little glum in here . . . We need plants. Lots of plants, from the floor to the ceiling. And sunshine. How do we get some sunshine in here?

GEORGE   I think our best bet is to wait for the morning.

   (He picks up her bags)

JENNIE   Oh, God! Humor! At last, humor!

GEORGE   Look, it's been a lousy day. And because of the time difference, we get an extra hour of lousy. Why don't we just write it off and go to bed.

JENNIE   I'm hungry.

GEORGE   *(Starts to unpack some tropical souvenirs)*   You just had dinner on the plane.

JENNIE   Airplane food is not dinner. It's survival. Come on, let's get a chili-burger.

GEORGE   I don't want one.

JENNIE   Don't be ridiculous. *Everybody* wants a chili-burger. Come on, George, a big, greasy, nongovernment-inspected burger dripping with illegal Mexican chili.

   (She gooses him with the Coke bottle)

GEORGE   *(Pulls away angrily)*   Cut it out, dammit!

JENNIE   *(Startled by his sudden hostility)*   I'm sorry.

GEORGE   How many times do I have to tell you? I don't want a goddamn chili hamburger!

JENNIE   Chili-*burger*. The ham is silent, like Hyphen Hill.

GEORGE Oh, very good. Give the girl two gallons of wine and the repartee really gets quick.

JENNIE Well, never as quick as you, George. Ah'm jes a dumb ole country girl from Cleveland.

GEORGE I noticed. Sitting on the plane with pen poised over the *New York Times* crossword puzzle for three and a half hours without ink ever *once* touching paper.

JENNIE I'm sorry, George. Am I not "literary" enough for you? How's this? "Up your syntax!"

GEORGE Swell. I'll try it tonight. I've been looking for a thrill.
(He goes into the kitchen. She sits, angry now, trying to figure out how to handle all this. GEORGE *comes back in with a glass of water)*

JENNIE I've tried everything, including my funniest faces, to get a smile out of you since eight o'clock this morning.

GEORGE Why don't you try an hour of quiet?
(He pops a Tylenol)

JENNIE I tried it in Barbados and it turned into twenty-four hours of gloom.

GEORGE Listen, I'm walking a very fine line tonight. There are a lot of things I would like to say that would just get us both in trouble. I don't want to deal with it now. Let's just go to bed and hope that two extra-strength Tylenol can do all they claim to do. Okay?

(He starts to cross back into the bedroom)

JENNIE   I'd just as soon hear what you had to say.

GEORGE   I don't think you would.

JENNIE   Why don't you be in charge of saying it and I'll be responsible for not wanting to hear it.

(He looks at her, nods, then looks around and decides to sit opposite her. She looks at him. He stares at the floor)

GEORGE   As honeymoons go, I don't think you got much of a break.

JENNIE   Really? I'm sorry if you felt that way. *I* had an intermittently wonderful time.

GEORGE   Well, I don't know what you experienced in the past. I'm not a honeymoon expert, but personally I found me unbearably moody.

JENNIE   Two days in seven isn't much of a complaint —which I never did. And I think we ought to limit this conversation to present honeymoons.

GEORGE   Why?

JENNIE   Because that's where we're living.

GEORGE   You can't get to the present without going through the past.

JENNIE   Jesus, George, is that what you did in Barbados? Compare honeymoons?

GEORGE   *(Stares at her)*   Why don't you ever ask me questions, Jennie? Why do you treat our lives as though there never was a day that happened before we met?

JENNIE   I'm not overly curious, George. If there are things you want to tell me, then tell me ... but *Christ*, does it have to be our first night in this house?

GEORGE   Jesus, I was wondering when that perfectly calm exterior was going to crack. Thank God for a little antagonism.

JENNIE   Antagonism, hell. That's pure fear. We haven't even started this conversation yet and I'm scared to death.

GEORGE   Why?

JENNIE   I have terrific animal instincts. I know when my life is about to be threatened.

GEORGE   Aren't you even curious to know who the hell we are? I mean, I think you've got some goddamn romantic image of this man with a tragic past right out of *Jane Eyre*.

JENNIE   You're the one with the writer's imagination, not me.

GEORGE   All right, I'll start. Who is Gus? I would appreciate some biographical information on the man

99

you spent a few important years of your life on. I
mean, he's got to be more than a comic figure in a
football jersey who pops up in a conversation every
time we need a laugh.

JENNIE   I never thought of him as comic.

GEORGE   Really? Well, anyone who's described as
pulling the wine cork out of the bottle with his teeth
didn't seem like heavyweight material to me.

JENNIE   I wish to hell I knew what you're trying to get
at.

GEORGE   Oh, come on, Jennie. Tell me *some*thing—
anything . . . What was your honeymoon like?
Would you say your sex life was A) good; B) bad; or
C) good and bad. Pick one!

JENNIE   Why are you doing this to me? I don't understand. Do you expect me to stand there and give a
detailed description of what it was like in bed with
him? Is that what you want to hear?

GEORGE   Okay, Jennie, forget it.

JENNIE   If you want the truth, I don't think I ever
knew the first damn thing about sex, because what
happened to you and me in Barbados was something
I never dreamed was possible. I hope you felt the
same way, George. You never gave me any cause to
doubt it . . . I'm sorry. This is very painful for me
to talk about . . . But I'll try, George, I'll try anything that's going to make us move closer to each
other.

GEORGE   I said forget it.

JENNIE   *(Yells)*   No, *goddammit!* You're not going to open me up and walk away from it. I went through one marriage ignorant as hell. At least let me learn from *this* one. What else? *Ask me!*

GEORGE   You're doing fine on your own.

JENNIE   Please, George. I'm not going to blow five years of analysis in one night because you haven't got the nerve to finish what you've started. I've always had problems with confrontations. If my father just looked at me with a curve in his eyebrow I fell apart. But I swear to God, I'm going to get through this one. *(He tries to leave the room; she blocks his way)* No other questions? *(He doesn't answer)* Then can I ask you a few?

GEORGE   Why not?

JENNIE   Tell me about Barbara.

GEORGE   *(Looks at her)*   She was terrific.

JENNIE   Oh, I know she was pretty. I see enough pictures of her around here. Tell me about your honeymoon. You went to Europe, didn't you?

GEORGE   Paris, London and Rome. And if you want a romantic description, it was a knockout.

JENNIE   I got the adjectives, George, what about the details? Big room? small room? view of the park? overlooking the Seine? fourposter bed? What was the wallpaper like?

GEORGE   Stop it, Jennie!

JENNIE   Why? What's wrong? Would you rather make out a list? What's safe to talk about and what's hands-off?

GEORGE *(A deep breath)*   Jesus, I don't have the strength for this kind of thing anymore.

JENNIE   You were doing fine two minutes ago.

GEORGE *(Looks at his hands)*   Sweating like crazy . . . I'm sorry, Jennie, I don't think I'm up to this tonight.

JENNIE   Why, George? Why is it so painful? What are you feeling now? Do you think that I'm expecting you to behave a certain way?

GEORGE   No. *I* expect it. I expect a full commitment from myself . . . I did it twelve years ago . . . But I can't do it now.

JENNIE   I'm in no hurry. What you're giving now is enough for me. I know the rest will come.

GEORGE   *How* do you know? How the hell did you become so wise and smart? Stop being so goddamn understanding, will you? It bores the crap out of me.

JENNIE   Then what *do* you want? Bitterness? Anger? Fury? You want me to stand toe to toe with you like Barbara did? Well, I'm not Barbara. And I'll be damned if I'm going to re-create *her* life, just to make *my* life work with you. This is *our* life now, George, and the sooner we start accepting that, the sooner we can get on with this marriage.

GEORGE   No, you're not Barbara. That's clear enough.

JENNIE *(Devastated)*   Oh, Jesus, George. If you want to hurt me, you don't have to work that hard.

GEORGE   Sorry, but you give me so much room to be cruel, I don't know when to stop.

JENNIE   I never realized that was a *fault* until now.

GEORGE   I guess it's one of the minor little adjustments you have to make. But I have no worry— you'll make them.

JENNIE   And you resent me for that?

GEORGE   I resent you for *everything!*

JENNIE *(Perplexed)*   *Why*, George? *Why?*

GEORGE   Because I don't feel like making you happy tonight! I don't feel like having a wonderful time. I don't think I *wanted* a "terrifically wonderful" honeymoon! You want happiness, Jennie, find yourself another football player, will ya? I resent everything you want out of marriage that I've already had. And for making me reach so deep inside to give it to you again. I resent being at L or M and having to go back to A! And most of all, I resent not being able to say in front of you . . . that I miss Barbara so much.
(*He covers his eyes, crying silently.* JENNIE *has been cut so deeply, she can hardly react. She just sits there, fighting back her tears*) Oh, Christ, Jennie, I'm sorry . . . I think I need a little outside assistance.

JENNIE *(Nods)* What do you want to do?

GEORGE *(Shrugs)* I don't know . . . I don't want to make any promises I can't keep.

JENNIE Whatever you want.

GEORGE We got, as they say in the trade, problems, kid.

> *(He goes to her, embraces her head, then goes into the bedroom, leaving her stunned and alone. Dimout)*

SCENE 6

Her apartment. It is two days later, about three o'clock on a sunny afternoon. The living room is empty.

FAYE *comes in from the bedroom, wearing a sheet—and apparently nothing else. Her hair is disheveled. She is distraught.*

LEO SCHNEIDER *comes out of the bedroom, zipping up his pants. He is nude from the waist up.*

LEO I'm sorry.

FAYE Forget it.

LEO Don't be like that.

FAYE What *should* I be like?

LEO It was an important phone call. I *had* to take it.

FAYE It's not taking it that bothered me. It's *when* you took it I felt was badly timed.

LEO Half my year's gross income depended on that call. He's my biggest client. Come on back . . . Faye? What do you say? They won't call again.

FAYE You mean you actually left this number? I changed taxis three times and walked with a limp into the building and you gave out this number?

LEO   It's just a number. It could be a luncheonette. He doesn't know. Faye, that phone call meant thirty thousand dollars to me.

FAYE   Jesus—I'm worried I'm going to be emotionally scarred for life, and you're getting rich.

LEO   You're so tense, Faye. You've been tense since I walked in the door. I knew when I came in and we shook hands, things weren't going to be relaxed.

FAYE   I'm no good at this, Leo. I'm nervous and I'm clumsy.

LEO   Don't be silly. You've been wonderful.

FAYE   I'm sorry about your shoes.

LEO   It's just a little red wine. They're practically dry.

FAYE   Your socks too?

LEO   Don't worry about it . . . Hey, Faye—Faysie! Have I offended you in some way? Have I been inconsiderate? Insensitive?

FAYE   Aside from adultery, you've been a perfect gentleman. I don't know . . . I just didn't think it would be so complicated. So noisy.

LEO   Noisy? What noise?

FAYE   My heart. It's pounding like a cannon. They must hear it all over the building.

LEO   I'll turn on the radio, they'll think it's the rhythm section . . . Hey! Would you like to dance?

FAYE   Are you serious?

LEO   Absolutely! You think it's corny? Well, I happen to be a very corny guy. Come on. Come dance with me.

FAYE   With red wine in your shoes? You'll squeak.

LEO *(Pulling* FAYE *to her feet)*   C'mon.
   (Singing)
   Flamingo . . .
   Like a flame in the sky . . .
   Flying over the island . . .
      (Taking her cigarette) Gimme that.
      (Singing)
   To my lover nearby . . .
      (Sings a scat phrase, starts dancing with FAYE)
   Hey, Flamingo . . .
   In your tropical hue . . .

FAYE   You're crazy, Leo.

LEO
   Words of passion and romance . . .

FAYE   You're embarrassing me.

LEO
   And my love for you . . .
      (Sings a scat phrase)
   One dip. Just give me one old-fashioned dip.
      (He dips her)

FAYE   Let me up, Leo. I'm in no mood to be dipped!
      (She slips a little and they slide to the floor)

LEO Jesus, you're pretty.

FAYE I'm not.

LEO Don't tell me you're not. I'm telling you you're pretty.

FAYE All right, I'm pretty. I don't want to argue.

LEO You're pretty and you're sweet and you've got the softest face.

FAYE You've done this a lot, haven't you, Leo?

LEO You get some particular thrill in dousing me with ice water?

FAYE You're so good at it. I admire your professionalism. It's all so well-crafted. Like a really well-built cabinet.

LEO Where do you find a parallel between my lovemaking and woodwork?

FAYE I may be new at this, Leo, but I'm not naïve. You've had affairs with married women before, haven't you?

LEO No . . .

FAYE Leo . . .

LEO There was one woman, but she was waiting for her divorce to come through.

FAYE A lot?

LEO Maybe one other.

FAYE   You've done it a lot.

LEO   A few times, I swear.

FAYE   A lot.

LEO   Yes, a lot. But they were never important to me. *Today* is important to me. *(Trying to caress her, he struggles with the sheet)* What is this tent you're wearing?

FAYE   *(She gets up, moves away)*   Please, Leo. A lot of meaningless affairs does not raise my appreciation of what we're doing.

LEO   It's not just the phone call that's bothering you. It's something else. You know what the problem is? You don't have a good enough reason to be here.

FAYE   That's a funny thing to say to a woman who shopped in twelve stores for the right underwear.

LEO   Well, then, maybe we rushed it. *I* rushed it, okay? Maybe this isn't the right time for you, Faye.

FAYE   What do *you* know about it? A couple of lousy affairs and you're suddenly Margaret Mead? Listen, when Jennie began having trouble with Gus, she decided to see an analyst. And I asked her, "When was the day you finally realized you needed one?" And she said, "It was the day I found myself in his office." Well, I'm *here* in your office . . . and I need something in my life. I already tried Transcendental Meditation, health foods and jogging. And I am now serenely, tranquilly and more robustly unhappy than I have ever been before . . . So don't tell me this isn't the right time, Sidney!

LEO   Leo.

FAYE   *Leo!* Oh, shit!

LEO   Oh, Faye, sweet Faye . . . You are so much more interesting-looking than you were twelve years ago. You've got so damn much character in your face.

FAYE   Why does that not overjoy me? Why is life going by so fast, Leo? First I was pretty. Now I'm interesting-looking with character! Soon I'll be handsome followed by stately and finally, worst of all, remarkable for her age.

LEO   Gloomy! You're taking a gloomy perspective, Faye. Gloom is the enemy of a good time.

FAYE   You were right before, Leo. I don't have a good enough reason to be here. Because what I want, I can't have. I want what Jennie has: the excitement of being in love again. I'm so much smarter now, I could handle everything so much better. I am so jealous of her I could scream. I did for her what I wish I could have done for myself. And in return I got her apartment to do exactly what I swore, when I was young and pretty, I would never end up doing when I became interesting-looking with character.

LEO   I think you're a very confused person, Faye.

FAYE   I've noticed that . . . I think you'd better leave first, Leo. I have to stay for a while and practice my limp.

LEO   I was crazy about you, Faysie . . . Never stopped thinking about you all through the years. I used to skim through the trades to see if you were working or not—

FAYE   Why didn't you ever try to get in touch with me?

LEO   I heard you were happily married.

FAYE   I heard you were, too.

LEO   Go trust people.

FAYE   I never told you this, but my mother didn't like you.

LEO   I never met her.

FAYE   I know, but I used to tell her about you. She said, "I know his type. He's the kind that needs lots of women.' I could call her and say, "You were right, Mom"—but how do I explain how I found out?

LEO   I wonder what would have happened if we had married each other?

FAYE   Well, I would hope a hell of a lot more than happened today . . . What's your opinion?

LEO   I think we'd have turned out swell.

FAYE You don't really believe that, do you?

LEO No.

FAYE Then why did you say it?

LEO I thought it would make you happy.

FAYE You're awful.

LEO Why? Because I want to please you? Are we better off deluding ourselves that ours would have been one of the great love affairs of midtown Manhattan? I know what it is and *you* know what it is —why do we have to call it something we both know it isn't?

FAYE Because a woman *needs* delusion.

LEO *(Putting on the rest of his clothes)* Not me. I need something new. It's why I like show business. There's another opening every three weeks. I can't be monogamous, Faye. What can I do, take shots for it? But in our system I'm put down as a social criminal. I can't be faithful to my wife, and I hate the guilt that comes with playing around. So I compromise. I have lots of unpleasurable affairs. And what makes it worse—I really do care for Marilyn. I can't stop, and I don't expect her to understand. So we end up hurting each other. I don't like it, Faye. I don't like crawling into bed at two o'clock in the morning and feeling the back of a cold, angry woman. And I don't like you coming up here under any false pretenses. I would love to make love to you, but that's the end of the sentence. I don't want a fine romance. I don't want to dance on the ceiling or have my heart stand still when "she" walks in the door. Because I really don't want to hurt anyone anymore. All I want is a little dispassionate passion . . . Let George and Jennie handle all the romance for the East Coast. The man is half-crazed right now, and he's welcome to it . . . I'll tell you what I *do* want, Faye. I want a woman who looks exactly like you and feels like you and thinks exactly like me.

FAYE   Boy, did I ever come to the wrong store to shop.

LEO   So what have we got here? We got one romantic unhappy woman, one indifferent frustrated man and one available and unused bedroom . . . is what we got here.

FAYE   It's too bad. You finally got me in the mood, and your honesty got me right out of it.

LEO   Anyway, I like you too much. Making love to people you like is very dangerous.

FAYE   Good. Save it for your enemies.

LEO *(Looks at his watch)*   Well, I can still get some work done. Can I drop you downtown?

FAYE   You mean, leave together? Suppose someone sees us?

LEO   Listen, they could have seen us in bed and never suspected anything. Come on, get dressed.

FAYE Leo, as a lover, you make a terrific friend. Would you mind giving me one warm, passionate and very sincere kiss? I'll be goddamned if I'm going home empty-handed.

LEO *(Steps toward her)* Hold on to your sheet, kid, kissing is my main thing.
> *(He gently puts his arms around her and gives her a soft, warm kiss on the lips. She pulls back, looks at him, and then suddenly feeling very safe, she leans forward again and they kiss deeply and passionately. His hands start to roam over her back. He gently puts her down on the sofa and begins to kiss her neck and her face as . . . the door opens and* JENNIE *walks in. She sees them and freezes)*

JENNIE Oh, God! I *am* sorry!
> *(They both jump up.* LEO *backs away)*

FAYE Oh, Jesus!

LEO Oh, Christ!

JENNIE I should have called. I didn't think—

LEO It's all right. It's okay. No harm done. We're all adults. It's a grown-up world. These things happen. We have to be mature—

FAYE Oh, shut up, Leo.

JENNIE I just came by to pick up the rest of my summer clothes. I can do it later. I'm so sorry.
> *(She backs up toward the door)*

FAYE   Don't think, Jennie. Don't think until I talk to you tonight. Promise me you won't think.

JENNIE   I won't. I promise . . . Goodbye, Leo. Say hello to Maril—! Goodbye, Leo!
(She turns and goes out, closing the door)

FAYE   This is one of those situations in life that a lot of people find humor in—I don't!
(She goes into the bedroom)

LEO   That's a first for me. That has never happened before. Never caught by a sister-in-law. *Never!*
(He leaves, slamming the front door)

His apartment, about an hour later. GEORGE *comes out of the bedroom, wearing a sports jacket and carrying a raincoat and fully packed suitcase and attaché case. He puts a note on the desk and starts for the door.*

JENNIE *enters, looking a little glum, sees* GEORGE *and his luggage.*

GEORGE Hi.

JENNIE Hi.

GEORGE You had some messages. *(Takes the piece of notepaper from the desk)* I was going to leave this for you. I don't know if you can read my writing ... Jill James at CBS called and said you start shooting again on Monday. They'll send the pages over to-night. Also, Helen Franklyn called and said you have a reading for the new Tom Stoppard play Monday at ten. And Faye called a few minutes ago, said it was urgent she talk to you and can you have lunch with her on Tuesday, Wednesday, Thursday and Friday . . . And that was it.

JENNIE *(Stunned; doesn't respond immediately)* I'm sorry, I wasn't listening . . . I couldn't take my eyes off your suitcase.

GEORGE I tried to explain everything in a letter. I left it on the bed.

JENNIE   Good. I was worried that I wasn't getting any mail . . . Where are you going?

GEORGE   Los Angeles. Someone at Paramount is interested in *The Duchess of Limehouse* as a film.

JENNIE   When did all this come up?

GEORGE   Two weeks ago.

JENNIE   Why didn't you tell me?

GEORGE   I had no reason to go two weeks ago.

JENNIE   Leave it to you to make a point clear. How long will you be gone?

GEORGE   I don't know.

JENNIE   Where will you stay?

GEORGE   I don't know.

JENNIE   Just going to circle the airport for a few days?

GEORGE   You never lose your equilibrium, do you?

JENNIE   You think not? I'd hate to see an X-ray of my stomach right now.

GEORGE   I don't think being apart for a while is going to do us any damage.

JENNIE   Probably no worse than being together the past few days.

GEORGE   But if it's really important to get in touch with me, Leo will know where I am.

JENNIE   And I'll know where Leo is.

GEORGE   *(Goes to the door, turns back uncomfortably)*   I don't think I have anything else to say. How about you?

JENNIE   *(Shrugs)*   I have no statement to make at this time.

GEORGE   I'm glad a lot of work is coming your way. I know it's important to you. It's what you want.

JENNIE   I'm glad you know what I want, George . . . If you told me five years ago, I could have saved a lot of doctor money.

GEORGE   I was busy five years ago.

JENNIE   You don't have to remind me. Interesting how this all worked out. You pack up and go and leave *me* with all your memories.

GEORGE   I'm sorry, but you can't get a five-room apartment in the overhead rack.

JENNIE   Is there anything you want me to take care of while you're gone?

GEORGE   You seem to be taking care of it fine right now.

JENNIE   Oh, I tripped over the wire and set off the trap, didn't I? . . . Everything I say can be so cleverly twisted around by you that you always end up the victim and I'm the perpetrator. God forbid I'm not as fast with a thought or a phrase as you, and you pounce on it like a fat cat.

GEORGE Fat cats are very slow on the pounce because they're fat, but I got your point.

JENNIE *(Very angry)* Oh, go on, get the hell out of here, will you! If you're going to leave, leave! Go! Your Mystery Plane is waiting to take you, shrouded in secrecy, to your Phantom Hotel on the intriguing West Coast. Even your life is turning into a goddamn spy novel—

GEORGE *(Puts down the valise)* I've got a few minutes. I don't want to miss what promises to be our most stimulating conversation since I thought you were an eighty-five-year-old woman on the phone.

JENNIE Isn't it amazing the minute I get angry and abusive, it's one of the few times I can really hold your attention . . . What can I say that will really hurt you, George? I want to send you off happy.
(She swarms over him, punching him. He throws her onto the sofa)

GEORGE Just going is reward enough.
(He starts out. She runs ahead of him and grabs the suitcase to fling it out. He throws her to the floor)

JENNIE You know what you want better than me, George . . . I don't know what you expect to find out there, except a larger audience for your two shows a day of suffering . . . I know I'm not as smart as you. Maybe I can't analyze and theorize and speculate on

119

why we behave as we do and react as we do and suffer guilt and love and hate. You read all those books, not me . . . But there's one thing I *do* know. I know how I *feel*. I know I can stand here watching you try to destroy everything I've ever wanted in my life, wanting to smash your face with my fists because you won't even make the slightest effort to opt for happiness—and still know that I love you. That's always so clear to me. It's the one place I get all my strength from . . . You mean so much to me that I am willing to take all your abuse and insults and insensitivity—because that's what you need to do to prove I'm not going to leave you. I can't promise I'm not going to die, George, that's asking too much. But if you want to test me, go ahead and test me. You want to leave, leave! But *I'm* not the one who's going to walk away. I don't know if I can take it forever, but I can take it for tonight and I can take it next week. Next month I may be a little shaky . . . But I'll tell you something, George. No matter what you say about me, I feel so good about myself —better than I felt when I ran from Cleveland and was frightened to death of New York. Better than I felt when Gus was coming home at two o'clock in the morning just to change his clothes. Better than I felt when I thought there was no one in the world out there for me, and better than I felt the night before we got married and I thought that I wasn't good enough for you . . . Well, I am! I'm wonderful! I'm nuts about me! And if you're stupid enough to throw someone sensational like me aside, then you don't deserve as good as you've got! I am sick and tired of running from places and people and relationships . . . And don't tell me what I want because *I'll* tell you what I want. I want a home and I want a family—and I want a career, too. And I want a dog and I want a cat and I want three goldfish. I want *everything*! There's no harm in wanting it, George, because there's not a chance in hell we're going to get it all, anyway. But if you don't *want* it, you've got even less chance than that . . . Everyone's out there looking for easy answers. And if you don't find it at home, hop into another bed and maybe you'll come up lucky. *Maybe!* You'd be just as surprised as me at some of the "maybe's" I've seen out there lately. Well, none of that for me, George . . . You want me, then fight for me, because I'm fighting like hell for you. I think we're both worth it. I will admit, however, that I *do* have one fault. One glaring, major, monumental fault . . . Sometimes I don't know when to stop talking. For that I'm sorry, George, and I apologize. I am now through!

(*She sits back on the sofa, exhausted*)

GEORGE (*Looks at her for a long time, then says warmly*) I'll tell you one thing—I'm glad you're on *my* side.

JENNIE (*Looks over at him*) Do you mean it, George?

GEORGE I didn't hear half of what you said because I was so mesmerized by your conviction. I'm not a doctor, Jennie, but I can tell you right now, you're one of the healthiest people I ever met in my life.

JENNIE *(Smiles)* Funny, I don't look it.

GEORGE I am crazy about you. I want you to know that.

JENNIE I know that.

GEORGE No. You don't know that I'm absolutely crazy nuts for you.

JENNIE Oh. No, I didn't know that. You're right.

GEORGE I want to walk over now and take you in my arms and say, "Okay, we're finished with the bad part. Now, what's for dinner?" But I'm stuck, Jennie . . . I'm just stuck someplace in my mind and it's driving me crazy. Something is keeping me here, glued to this spot like a big, dumb, overstuffed chair.

JENNIE I could rearrange the furniture.

GEORGE Don't make it so easy for me. I'm fighting to hold on to self-pity, and just my luck I run into the most understanding girl in the world.

JENNIE I'm not so understanding.

GEORGE Yes, you are. You just said so yourself. And I swear to God, Jennie, I can't find a thing I would want to change about you . . . So let me go to Los Angeles. Let me try to get unstuck . . . I'll be at the Chateau Marmont Hotel. I'll be in my room un-sticking like crazy.

JENNIE   Couldn't I go with you? I wouldn't bother you. I would just watch.

GEORGE   Then the people next door would want to watch, and pretty soon we'd have a crowd. *(He picks up his suitcase)* Take care of yourself.

JENNIE   George! *(He stops, looks at her)* Would you mind very much if I slept in my apartment while you're gone? I feel funny about staying in this place alone.

GEORGE   *(Nods)*   I understand . . .

JENNIE   If you don't call me, can I call you?

GEORGE   *(A pause)*   You know, we may have one of the most beautiful marriages that was ever in trouble.
   (He goes out. She goes to the door, watches him go, then comes in and closes the door. Dimout)

Her apartment. The next day. The doorbell rings. FAYE *opens the door. It is* LEO.

LEO Oh? Hello! Do I look as surprised as you?

FAYE What are you doing here?

LEO I just dropped by.

FAYE To see me?

LEO No.

FAYE Thank God. I was afraid it was one of those habits you can't break.

LEO Is Jennie home?

FAYE She's in the shower. She moved back last night . . . So much for our matchmaking business.

LEO Actually I came back hoping to find my wallet. I think I dropped it in the bedroom yesterday during the mass exodus.

FAYE Jennie found it. She woke up in the middle of the night with a credit card lump under her head.
(She gives him a small Manila envelope, held with a rubber band. He looks at it)

LEO She didn't have to put my name on it. It's humiliating enough. Did she say anything about us?

FAYE That's not her style . . . I was prepared to tell her I'd been drugged. You don't mind, do you?

LEO Look, why don't we just write off yesterday? Even my horoscope said, "Stay outdoors."

FAYE I'm in the process of forgetting about it. I'm seeing Jennie's old doctor on Monday.

LEO That's terrific. I'm glad you're doing something constructive about your problems.

FAYE And what about you, Leo? What are you doing?

LEO (Shrugs) Nothing! I have no intention of changing. So why should I pay some doctor to make me feel guilty about it?

FAYE And what about you and Marilyn? Are you going to separate?

LEO Yes. But not this year. We have too many dinner dates . . . (He stands) Well, I'll see you around, kid.

FAYE Every place but here.

LEO Keep your options open. It makes life more interesting.

FAYE Why is it the more you say things I don't like, the more attractive you get?

LEO That's what's going to cost you fifty bucks an hour to find out . . . We never did finish that warm, passionate, friendly kiss.

FAYE   You know what? I think I'm just crazy enough to do it.

> (*They kiss.* JENNIE *walks in from the bedroom in a bathrobe, drying her hair with a towel*)

JENNIE   Faye, was that the phone I heard befo—? (*She stops, seeing them. They break apart*) Jesus, is that the same kiss from yesterday?

LEO   My regiment was just called up and I'm trying to say goodbye to everybody . . . Maybe next week the three of us can meet in a restaurant, because I'd like to explain this whole silly business. We'll all wear hoods, of course.

JENNIE   Leo . . . Have you heard from George?

LEO   No . . . but give him a couple of days, Jen. He'll figure it out. (*Kisses her, starts out, stops*) Jesus, life was so simple when we were kids. No matter how much trouble you got into outside, when you got home you always got a cupcake.

> (*He leaves*)

FAYE   (*Looks sheepishly at* JENNIE)   I feel so foolish. Do you hate me?

JENNIE   (*Smiles*)   I could never hate you.

FAYE   Well, I have another confession to make to you . . . Leo was never the one I wanted to have an affair with.

JENNIE   Who was?

FAYE   A certain ex-wide receiver from the New York Giants.

JENNIE   *Gus?*

FAYE   I lusted for that man in more places than my heart.

JENNIE   Then why did you pick Leo?

FAYE   Because I was intimate with him before I met Sidney . . . I just wanted to practice with someone I already knew.

JENNIE   You have a peculiar bookkeeping system.

FAYE   Anyway, Sidney and I are going to an adult motel in New Jersey this weekend. From now on, I'm only cheating with the immediate family . . . I've got to go. Are you sure you'll be all right? I mean, staying here all alone?

JENNIE   Wait a minute. Am I having a déjà vu or have we played this scene before?

FAYE   The dialogue *does* seem awfully familiar. I remember saying, "Shit. Twelve more years to go until the good times" and then falling in love with the girl across the street.

JENNIE   Oh, God. Our life is on a loop. Does this mean I have to go out with the giant from Chicago again?

FAYE   I'd better go before Leo comes in with a bottle of red wine. *(She crosses to the door, opens it, then turns back)* There's a lesson to be learned from all this . . . I wonder what the hell it is.
   (She leaves. Fadeout)

His apartment. The door opens. GEORGE *enters and turns on the lights. He looks a little travel-weary.*

GEORGE *(Putting down his suitcase)* Jennie? Jennie?
  (He looks around, then goes into the bedroom. It's apparent no one is home. He comes back into the living room. In her apartment, JENNIE *goes to the refrigerator, takes out an apple, then goes to the sofa and sits.* GEORGE *picks up the phone, and starts to dial just as* JENNIE *picks up the receiver. She dials 213-555-1212. He finishes dialing and gets a busy signal. He hangs up, takes a manuscript from his attaché case)*

JENNIE *(Into the phone)* Los Angeles . . . I'd like the number of the Chateau Marmont Hotel . . . Yes, I think it *is* West Hollywood . . . *(She waits. He paces)* 656–1010 Thank you. *(She disconnects with her finger, then starts to dial just as he goes back to the phone, picks it up and starts to dial. She gets halfway through the number when she suddenly hangs up)* Patience, Jennie! Don't pressure him. *(She sits back just as he completes his dial. Her phone rings. She jumps and clutches her bosom)* Oh, God, I'm so smart! *(She reaches over and picks up the phone)* Hello?

GEORGE Serene?

JENNIE Who?

GEORGE Is this Serene Jurgens? . . . It's George Schneider, Leo's brother . . . I just arrived on the Coast, darling. At last, I'm free.

JENNIE *(Near tears)* Tell me you're joking, George. Right now I wouldn't know humor if it hit me with a truck.

GEORGE Oh. Well, then you'd better pull off the highway . . . How are you? What have you been doing?

JENNIE Watching the telephone. Nothing good on until now . . . How's the weather there?

GEORGE *(Looks around)* Oh, about eighty-four degrees. A little humid.

JENNIE Same here . . . How are you, George?

GEORGE Dumb. Dummy Dumbo.

JENNIE Why?

GEORGE Well, when Barbara and I had a fight, I'd walk around the block and come back twenty minutes later feeling terrific . . . At the airport I said to myself, "Of course. That's what I should do." And that's what I did.

JENNIE I can't believe it. You mean, you just walked around the block?

GEORGE Yes.

JENNIE   What's so dumb about that?

GEORGE   I was in the Los Angeles airport when I thought of it.

JENNIE   Well, where are you? Here or there?

GEORGE   Wait, I'll look. *(He looks around)* Looks like here.

JENNIE   You're back! You're in New York!

GEORGE   I never even checked into the Chateau Marmont . . . I got unstuck in the TWA lounge.

JENNIE   Oh, George . . .

GEORGE   I sat there drinking my complimentary Fresca, and I suddenly remembered a question Dr. Ornstein told me to ask myself whenever I felt trouble coming on. The question is "What is it you're most afraid would happen *if?*"

JENNIE   I'm listening.

GEORGE   So I said to myself, "George, what is it you're most afraid would happen—*if* you went back to New York . . . to Jennie . . . and started your life all over again?" And the answer was so simple . . . I would be happy! I have stared happiness in the face, Jennie—and I embrace it.

JENNIE   *(Tearfully)*   Oh, George. You got any left to embrace me?

GEORGE   From here? No. You need one of those long-armed fellas for that.

JENNIE Well, what are we waiting for? Your place or mine?

GEORGE Neither. I think we have to find a new one called "Ours."

JENNIE Thank you, George. I was hoping we would.

GEORGE Thus, feeling every bit as good about me as you do about you, I finished the last chapter of the new book on the plane. *(He takes up the manuscript. The last few pages are handwritten)* I've got it with me. You want to hear it?

JENNIE The last chapter?

GEORGE No. The whole book.

JENNIE Of course. I'll be right over.

GEORGE No, I'll read it to you. I don't want to lose my momentum. *(He opens the manuscript folder, settles back; so does she. He reads)* You ready? . . . *Falling Into Place*, by George Schneider. Dedication: "To Jennie . . . A nice girl to spend the rest of your life with . . ." *(He turns the page)* Chapter One . . . "Walter Maslanski looked in the mirror and saw what he feared most . . . Walter Maslanski . . ." *(The curtain begins to fall)* "Not that Walter's features were awesome by any means . . . He had the sort of powder-puff eyes that could be stared down in an abbreviated battle by a one-eyed senior-citizen canary . . ."

Curtain

Since 1960, a Broadway season without a Neil Simon comedy or musical has been a rare one. During the 1966–67 season, *Barefoot in the Park, The Odd Couple, Sweet Charity* and *The Star-Spangled Girl* were all running simultaneously; in the 1970–71 season, Broadway theatergoers had their choice of *Plaza Suite, Last of the Red Hot Lovers* and *Promises, Promises*. Next came *The Prisoner of Second Avenue, The Sunshine Boys, The Good Doctor, God's Favorite, California Suite* and *Chapter Two*.

Mr. Simon began his writing career in television and has now established himself as our leading writer of comedy by creating a succession of Broadway hits. He has also written for the screen: the adaptations of *Barefoot in the Park, The Odd Couple, Plaza Suite, The Prisoner of Second Avenue* and *The Sunshine Boys;* and the original screenplays *The Out-of-Towners, The Heartbreak Kid* and *Murder by Death*. His latest films are *The Goodbye Girl* and *The Cheap Detective*.

By his own analysis, "Doc" Simon has always been "that person sitting in the corner who's observing it all" for all of his fifty years, an insight he explores in his introduction entitled "Portrait of the Writer as a Schizophrenic," written for the anthology of his plays published by Random House. That volume, *The Comedy of Neil Simon*, is a tribute to the brilliance of its author, as are the Tony Award he received for Best Playwright of 1965 and his selection as *Cue* magazine's Entertainer of the Year for 1972.